Contents

Act 1 Scene 1

You must be able to: understand what happens at the beginning of the play and how Delaney establishes the setting and the relationships between the characters.

What is the setting?

The opening stage direction says the play is set in 'a comfortless flat in Manchester and the street outside'. In fact, it is set in a run-down area of neighbouring Salford. The flat has a living room, a bedroom with one bed and (off-stage) a kitchen. Jo and Helen share a bathroom with tenants of other flats.

Who are the characters?

Jo is still at school but anxious to leave and get a job. She is 16 or 17. Helen is her mother. She is about 40. She has been married but has also had a lot of boyfriends. She is described in the stage directions as 'a semi-whore'. In the past she has worked in a pub.

How does the play begin?

Helen and Jo enter with luggage. It is clear that they are moving into the flat and that they move often but it is not clear where they have come from or why they have moved this time.

Jo is not impressed with the flat and, by implication, Helen, who says it is all she can afford. Jo tries to make it look better by hanging a scarf over the naked light bulb while her mother, who has a cold, drinks whisky. Jo goes to the kitchen to make coffee.

Jo produces some flower bulbs which she has stolen from the park. Helen asks her whether she 'still intends to leave school at Christmas' and she says that she does. Helen reminisces about her first job in a pub and sings. She admires some drawings that Jo has done. Jo says that she is going to have a bath.

What changes the situation?

Peter, 'a brash car salesman' and Helen's boyfriend, enters. It is apparent that Helen has left him and did not give him the new address but he has tracked her down. Jo has never met him before and is hostile towards him. Helen is also hostile at first but her attitude softens and they flirt. He asks Helen to marry him but she does not give him an answer.

What happens at the end of the scene?

Peter leaves. Jo says that she has changed her mind about having a bath because she is afraid of the 'darkness inside houses'. Helen and Jo go to bed.

Key Quotations to Learn

Helen: Well! This is the place.
Jo: And I don't like it.

Helen: What are you going to do?
Jo: Get out of your sight as soon as I get a bit of money in my pocket.

Jo: What about me? Don't you think I get fed up with all this flitting about?

Summary

- Jo and Helen move into a small, run-down flat.
- Jo wants something better but Helen says it is all they can afford.
- Helen's boyfriend, Peter, turns up and asks Helen to marry him.
- Helen does not give him an answer and he leaves.
- Jo and Helen go to bed.

Questions

QUICK TEST
1. What is Jo's reaction to the flat?
2. What does Jo do to try to make the flat more attractive?
3. What does Jo intend to do at Christmas?
4. Who is Peter?

EXAM PRACTICE
Using at least one of the 'Key Quotations to Learn', write a paragraph analysing how Delaney establishes the relationship between Jo and Helen in Act 1 Scene 1.

Act 1 Scene 2

You must be able to: understand what happens in Act 1 Scene 2.

When and where is Act 1 Scene 2 set?

Scene 2 takes place a few weeks or months after Scene 1, not long before Christmas. It can be seen as four separate scenes. The first takes place in the street outside the flat. The other three take place in the flat.

What happens in the first part of Act 1 Scene 2?

Jo is walking home from school with 'the Boy'. He is described in the stage directions as 'a coloured naval rating'.

The Boy kisses Jo and she resists him. He suggests that she might not want to be seen with him, revealing his awareness of their being an inter-racial couple, but she says she does not care. He asks her to marry him and she agrees. They say that they love each other. He gives her a ring and they make plans to marry when he is next on leave – in six months' time.

Jo reveals that she will be leaving school that week and has a part-time job in a bar. He says he cannot see her that night but they agree to meet the following day.

Jo waves goodbye to the Boy who sings to the audience before exiting. Helen enters the flat and lies down, reading the paper. Jo moves from 'the street' into the flat.

What happens in the second part of the scene?

Jo tells Helen a bit about the Boy and asks Helen about her father. Helen is reluctant to answer but does explain that her husband threw her out when she became pregnant by another man – Jo's father.

Peter enters with flowers and chocolates. While Helen is getting ready to go out, Jo and Peter argue and Jo attacks Peter. When Helen comes back on stage, she tells Jo that Peter has bought a house. After she goes off again, Jo once more turns on Peter, quizzing him about his past. She demands to see the contents of his wallet. There are a lot of pictures of women.

When Helen returns, she says that she and Peter might go for a weekend in Blackpool. Jo asks for money. Helen accuses Jo of being jealous. She and Peter leave.

What happens in the second scene between Jo and the Boy?

Jo lies on the bed and cries. The Boy enters. He comforts her. Jo invites him to stay with her over Christmas. They talk about love. It is clear that Jo intends to have sex with the Boy. The lights fade out.

What happens in the final part of Act 1 Scene 2?

It is the day of Helen's wedding. Helen sees the ring around Jo's neck. When Jo tells her that she is engaged, Helen is angry, calling her stupid and saying she is ruining her life.

Jo again asks about her father and Helen describes him as 'a bit – retarded' but says he is now dead. Jo says that she is neither sorry nor glad that Helen is leaving. She also says that she knows what she wants from life but does not say what it is.

Key Quotations to Learn

Boy: Afraid someone'll see us?

Helen: … You jealous little cat!

Helen: I don't suppose you're sorry to see me go.
Jo: I'm not sorry and I'm not glad.

Summary

- Jo has started a relationship with 'the Boy', who asks her to marry him.
- Jo argues violently with Peter when he comes to collect Helen.
- The Boy comforts Jo and moves into the flat while Helen is away.
- Helen marries Peter and Jo is left alone in the flat.

Questions

QUICK TEST
1. What does the Boy think is the reason Jo does not want to kiss him?
2. What does Helen think is the reason for Jo's dislike of Peter?
3. Who stays in the flat over Christmas?
4. What is Helen's reaction to seeing Jo's ring?

EXAM PRACTICE
Using at least one of the 'Key Quotations to Learn', write a paragraph explaining how Jo reacts to Helen's relationship with Peter in Act 1 Scene 2.

You must be able to: understand what happens in Act 2 Scene 1.

When and where does Act 2 Scene 1 take place?

The first part of the scene is set in the summer and the second 'a month or two later'. The whole scene takes place in the flat.

What has changed between Act 1 and Act 2?

Jo is pregnant. She is now living in the flat alone and has two jobs. She has made friends with Geof, a gay art student.

What happens in the scene between Jo and Geof?

Jo and Geof arrive in the flat after a day out at the fair. Geof criticises the state of it. He has been thrown out of his flat and Jo invites him to stay. She is curious about his homosexuality but he thinks she is making fun of him and starts to leave. She apologises and persuades him to stay.

Geof criticises Jo's drawings. She says she has never been to art school and he responds that she needs 'taking in hand'. They discuss her pregnancy. Jo has not made any plans for the baby.

Geof thinks Jo is depressed. He cheers her up. Jo goes to bed and Geof goes to bed on the couch. Jo tells Geof about the Boy. Geof says he will clear up in the morning and make her a 'proper meal'.

What happens in the second part of Act 2 Scene 1?

Geof is busy making clothes for the baby. Jo is restless. She feels the baby kick.

Geof tells Jo a neighbour is making a wicker cradle for the baby. He gives her a book about bringing up babies but she laughs at it and says she hates motherhood. She asks him if he would like to be the father of her baby. He says he would. He kisses her and asks her to marry him. She rejects him but agrees that he should stay in the flat.

What happens when Helen arrives?

Helen has been asked to come over by Geof because he is worried about Jo. Jo and Helen immediately start arguing as Helen asks about Jo's living arrangements. Jo is no longer working and has no money. Helen says she has come to tell Jo 'some home truths'. When Geof accuses her of bullying Jo, they both turn on him. Helen gives Jo some money and offers to send more.

How does Peter's entrance change things?

Peter is drunk. He insults Jo and Geof. Helen asks Jo to come and live with her but Peter says he does not want 'that bloody slut at our place'. When he tells Helen to leave with him, she asks Jo if she would like her to stay. Jo says no and Helen leaves with Peter, who has taken back the money.

Key Quotations to Learn

Jo: Go on, I've always wanted to know about people like you.

Jo: You're just like a big sister to me.

Geof: She won't go out anywhere, not even for a walk and a bit of fresh air. That's why I came to you.

Summary

- It is summer and Jo is expecting a baby in September.
- Geof offers to look after her and moves into the flat.
- Geof asks Jo to marry him but she rejects him.
- Helen returns and, after arguing with Jo, gives her money.
- Helen invites Jo to live with her and Peter but Peter says he does not want Jo in his house.
- He takes back the money and they leave.

Questions

QUICK TEST
1. Which new character is introduced at the beginning of Act 2?
2. What subject is Geof studying?
3. Why does Helen come to see Jo?
4. What does Peter call Jo?

EXAM PRACTICE
Using at least one of the 'Key Quotations to Learn', write a paragraph explaining how Delaney explores the relationship between Jo and Geof in Act 2 Scene 1.

You must be able to: understand what happens in Act 2 Scene 2.

What is the situation at the beginning of Act 2 Scene 2?

It is more than a month since the last scene and Jo's baby is due very soon. Geof is still living with her.

What happens between Jo and Geof?

Geof is doing housework while Jo reads a book about pregnancy. Geof discovers the bulbs from Act 1 still under the couch. They have not grown. Jo becomes upset and nervous. Geof calms her. She tells him the story that her mother told her about her father but he does not believe it and convinces Jo that it is not true.

Geof gives Jo a doll to 'practise' on. She says it is the wrong colour before suddenly becoming angry and throwing it to the ground. She says that she does not want to be a mother and will kill her baby. Geof suggests she has it adopted. She does not respond to the suggestion. He asks if she still loves the father. She says she does not know and reveals that his name was Jimmie. She says that she is happy with Geof.

What happens next?

Helen arrives *'with baggage as in Act One'*. She expresses concern about Jo's welfare and asks if she has packed. Jo says she is not going to the hospital to have the baby. Helen claims that she has come to look after Jo and says she has brought things for the baby. She tells Geof to leave and insults him.

Jo questions Helen and finds out that Peter has gone off with another woman. Helen says that she thought she ought to be with Jo. Jo tells her that she feels 'important' for the first time in her life.

Geof returns with shopping, which Helen criticises. She also criticises the state of the flat and the wicker cot. She makes it clear that she wants Geof to leave. He asks her not to frighten Jo and says that Jo wants him at the birth, which Helen thinks is 'disgusting'. Helen again tells him to go. Saying that Jo could not cope with both him and Helen, Geof leaves.

How does the play end?

Helen and Jo are alone in the flat. Jo starts to have **contractions** and Helen comforts her, stroking her hair and talking about her own childhood. Jo tells her the baby 'will be black' and Helen is shocked at first but then jokes about it, suggesting the black nurse might adopt the child or they could 'put it on the stage'. Helen leaves the flat but tells Jo she will be coming back.

The ending is **ambiguous**. Jo is alone and the audience does not know whether Helen will stay with her or if Geof will return. However, Jo seems happy as she recites a nursery rhyme and *'remembers Geof'*.

Key Quotations to Learn

Jo: So we're back where we started.

Geof: I'm going. She can't cope with the two of us. Only just don't frighten her, that's all.

Helen: … I don't know what's to be done with you, I don't really. (*To the audience*) I ask you, what would you do?

Summary

- Geof tries to help Jo prepare for the birth of the baby.
- Jo's mood and her feelings about the baby change rapidly.
- Helen returns with her baggage, saying she will look after Jo.
- Helen tells Geof to leave and he does so.
- Jo tells Helen her baby may be black.

Questions

QUICK TEST
1. What does Geof think about Jo's story about her father?
2. How does Jo react to the doll?
3. Why have Helen and Peter split up?
4. What is Helen's reaction to hearing the baby might be black?

EXAM PRACTICE
Using at least one of the 'Key Quotations to Learn', write a paragraph about how the play ends.

Structure

You must be able to: understand how Delaney has structured the play.

How is the play organised?

The play is in two acts. There is usually an interval between them. There is one set, which is not changed between acts or scenes. All the action takes place in Jo's flat or the street outside.

In the published script, each act contains two scenes. Act 1 Scene 2 and Act 2 Scene 1 both contain shifts in time and place which are not formally marked as new scenes.

How does Delaney indicate shifts in time within scenes?

In the stage directions, Delaney sometimes indicates changes in lighting to mark time shifts. She also uses music and describes characters as 'dancing' on and off the set. This helps to make the action flow more smoothly.

How is the story structured?

The story follows Jo's life in **chronological order** over a period of about ten months from when she and Helen move into the flat to just before she gives birth. The plot is not complicated and does not contain any big surprises or shocks.

Act 1 Scene 1 is mainly **exposition** as the main characters, Jo and Helen, and the setting and situation are introduced to the audience. Things change with the introduction of Peter and his proposal to Helen.

There is a **turning point** in Act 1 Scene 2 when Helen leaves with Peter and the Boy moves in with Jo, ending the first act. It is the combination of these two events that changes Jo's life.

There is a jump of several months between Acts 1 and 2. Jo is now pregnant and Act 2 follows the later stages of her pregnancy. The introduction of Geof in Act 2 Scene 1 shifts the focus away from Jo's relationship with Helen – until Helen reappears.

The audience is aware that more than six months have passed and Jimmie (previously referred to as 'the Boy') has not returned as he promised.

Helen's return to the flat and Geof's departure in Act 2 Scene 2 provide a twist to the plot. Helen's return 'with baggage' also reminds the audience of the beginning of the play and how much has changed since then. This technique is called circular structure.

The plot does not build up to a dramatic climax but moves towards a natural conclusion with the imminent birth of the baby, signalled by Jo having a contraction. At the end of the play she is alone on stage.

The ending has been described as 'open' or ambiguous. This is because the audience is left wondering what will happen next. Will Helen stay with Jo? Will Geof return? What will Jo do with the baby after it is born? How will her life change?

Key Quotations to Learn

Enter HELEN, *a semi-whore, and her daughter,* JO. *They are loaded with baggage.* (Act 1 Scene 1)

It is summer now and JO's *pregnancy is quite obvious.* (Act 2 Scene 1)

HELEN *enters, loaded with baggage as in Act One, Scene One.* (Act 2 Scene 2)

Summary

- The play is divided into two acts, each with two scenes.
- Within two of these scenes there are shorter 'scenes' when there is a change of place or time.
- The play follows Jo's life in chronological order, from when she and Helen move into the flat to just before the birth of her baby.
- The play has a 'circular' structure as the situation at the end recalls the beginning.
- The ending is 'open', leaving the audience wondering what might happen next.

Questions

QUICK TEST
1. Which two characters are introduced to the audience at the start of the play?
2. Which two events change Jo's life in Act 1?
3. Over what period of time does the play take place?
4. Who is on stage at the end of the play?

EXAM PRACTICE
Using at least one of the 'Key Quotations to Learn', write a paragraph exploring the similarities and differences between the situation at the beginning and at the end of the play.

Shelagh Delaney and *A Taste of Honey*

You must be able to: understand how the play has been shaped by the author's life and the circumstances surrounding the writing of the play.

Who was Shelagh Delaney?

Shelagh Delaney (1938–2011) was born in Salford, Lancashire (now Greater Manchester). Her father, Frank, was a bus conductor. At the beginning of the Second World War he joined the army and Shelagh moved with her mother, Elsie, into her grandmother's house near the docks. After the war, the family was rehoused in a new council house. At 11, Shelagh went to a **secondary modern school** but was transferred to the local girls' grammar school at 14. She left school at 17 after two terms in the sixth form and did a number of different jobs, including working in a shop and in a factory where (like Jo) she touched up photographs.

Why did Delaney write *A Taste of Honey*?

Delaney began writing at school. Her desire to be a writer was one of her reasons for leaving school. She worked as an usherette at the Royal Opera House, Manchester, where she saw many plays. At around the same time, she joined the Salford Players, an amateur theatre group, and wrote sketches for them. She was encouraged by David Scase, director of the Manchester Library Theatre, who had formerly worked at the Theatre Workshop in London.

Delaney was influenced by writers such as Arthur Miller, whose *Death of A Salesman* she had seen on a school trip, and Samuel Beckett, whose *Waiting For Godot* she saw when working as an usherette. She was less impressed by *Variations on a Theme,* a play by Terence Rattigan, a successful writer who had been very popular but was going out of fashion. She saw it at the Opera House and found the upper-middle-class world it portrayed laughable. She decided that she could do better and, intending to put 'ordinary people' on stage, immediately started work on *A Taste of Honey*. She was 19 at the time.

How has Shelagh Delaney's background influenced the play?

Many people assumed that the character of Jo was based on Shelagh Delaney herself. In fact, Delaney's secure childhood was very different from Jo's. However, there are similarities. Jo's drawings indicate a vague desire to be creative that mirrors Shelagh's ambition to write. They also share an impatience with school and an inability to stick at a job.

How did people react to the play?

The play was an instant success with audiences. While many critics praised its freshness and authenticity, confirming that Delaney had succeeded in her ambition to put ordinary people on stage, some found the characters unpleasant. Some residents of Salford objected to her portrayal of their city. Delaney responded that her characters were not intended to be seen as typical or representative of the place.

Summary

- Delaney was born and grew up in Salford.
- She left school at 17, determined to be a writer.
- She thought theatre should reflect the lives of ordinary people.
- The character of Jo is similar to Shelagh Delaney in some ways but in other ways their lives are quite different.

Questions

QUICK TEST
1. Where was Shelagh Delaney born?
2. Which job did Delaney do that helped her learn about the theatre?
3. Which two playwrights influenced Delaney?
4. What was Delaney's response to accusations that her characters portrayed Salford in a bad light?

EXAM PRACTICE
Look at this **dialogue** from Act 2 between Helen and Jo:

Helen: Why, are you still set on leaving school at Christmas?

Jo: Yes.

Helen: What are you going to do?

Jo: Get out of your sight as soon as I can get a bit of money in my pocket.

Relating your ideas to the historical context, write a paragraph exploring how Delaney presents ideas about school in *A Taste of Honey*.

Joan Littlewood and the Theatre Workshop

You must be able to: understand the role played by Joan Littlewood in developing *A Taste of Honey* and the theatrical context of the time.

Who was Joan Littlewood and what was the Theatre Workshop?

Joan Littlewood (1914–2002) was a British theatre director. She wanted to make theatre more accessible and relevant to ordinary working-class people.

In 1945, she and her husband, folk singer Ewan MacColl, founded the Theatre Workshop as a touring company. In 1953, the company settled in the Theatre Royal, a Victorian theatre in Stratford, east London.

Littlewood put on classics and new plays. She used **improvisation** in rehearsal and to develop scripts. She was influenced by the German playwright Bertolt Brecht and interested in popular theatre forms such as **music hall**.

What was British theatre like in the 1950s?

The 1950s were a time of great change in the theatre. Writers such as Rattigan, whose play Delaney had found ridiculously old-fashioned, were still popular with audiences but increasingly disliked by critics, directors and new writers, who considered them **elitist** and irrelevant.

In 1956, John Osborne's play *Look Back in Anger* was produced at the Royal Court Theatre in London. It was seen as the beginning of a new movement in the theatre and more plays featuring working-class or lower-middle-class characters in realistic situations were produced. This style of theatre is often referred to as **'kitchen sink drama'**. Osborne and other new writers were called the **'Angry Young Men'**.

In some ways, Delaney's play can be seen as part of this movement although she differed in being a woman and in her own assertion that she was not angry.

How did Joan Littlewood influence *A Taste of Honey*?

In April 1958, Shelagh Delaney sent her play to Joan Littlewood. In an accompanying letter, designed to appeal to Littlewood, she claimed that she had never been to a theatre until two weeks earlier. Joan Littlewood decided to put on the play and Delaney went to London to work with her. Delaney's **public image** as an uneducated, northern, working-class writer (which she later resented) was soon established. This image, promoted by Littlewood, contributed to the play's success.

At the time, some critics thought that Littlewood had written the play, not believing that it could be the work of a teenage girl. In fact, most of the play was Delaney's work but Littlewood did make some changes. The character of Peter became much more unpleasant, for example, and Helen's reaction to finding out the baby 'will be black' was made more extreme. The ending was also changed: originally, Jo went into hospital to have the baby, with the intention of going to live with Helen and Peter, and Geof was left alone on stage. Delaney must have been happy with these changes as she did not take up the opportunity to reverse them for later productions.

The finished script and original staging also reflect the **Brechtian** style of the Theatre Workshop in the use of music, dance and direct address to the audience.

Summary

- Joan Littlewood wanted to bring theatre to working-class audiences.
- Theatre in the 1950s changed with the arrival of the 'Angry Young Men' and 'kitchen sink drama'.
- Littlewood immediately accepted *A Taste of Honey* and worked on it with Delaney.
- Littlewood's influence is apparent in some changes that she suggested and the style of the play.

Questions

QUICK TEST
1. Which German playwright influenced Littlewood?
2. What popular art form influenced Littlewood?
3. Which play started off the fashion for 'kitchen sink drama'?
4. Did Delaney consider herself an 'angry young woman'?

EXAM PRACTICE
Look at this extract from Act 1 Scene 1.

(Helen):   ...I used to bring the house down with this one. (*Sings*)
           I'd give the song birds to the wild wood
           I'd give the sunset to the blind
           And to the old folks I'd give the memory
             of the baby upon their knee.
[*To orchestra*]:   Come on, vamp it in with me.

Relating your ideas to the context, write a paragraph explaining how this extract reflects the **house style** of the Theatre Workshop.

Set and Staging

You must be able to: comment on how the staging of the play tells us about themes and characters.

What are stage directions for?

Stage directions are there to help directors and actors understand how to perform a play. Sometimes they indicate where and when a scene is happening. Sometimes they tell the actors what to do. Brief directions, placed in brackets after a character's name, indicate what the actor is doing while speaking or how he or she should deliver a line.

How should stage directions be written about?

Think about the effect of the stage directions. How do they affect the mood and atmosphere? How do they show what the characters are thinking or feeling?

When writing about a play, remember that it is a script to be performed and may be interpreted differently by different actors and directors. For example, some productions might not use music and lighting in the way described in the script.

Stage directions can be quoted in your essays in the same way as dialogue.

How does Delaney describe the set?

There is one set, which remains unchanged throughout the play. Delaney does not give a detailed description, only stating that it 'represents a comfortless flat … and the street outside'. It is up to the designer and director to decide how to represent these two areas and how actors pass from one to the other.

Some productions might opt for a very **naturalistic** set, making the flat look as much like a real flat as possible. However, the stage directions – which reflect the style of the original production and are probably Joan Littlewood's work – suggest a set that is not entirely naturalistic and is more in keeping with the Theatre Workshop's preferred Brechtian style.

What is meant by Brechtian theatre?

During the nineteenth and early twentieth centuries, most theatre tried to imitate real life, with naturalistic sets and acting, reinforced by the **convention** of the 'fourth wall', meaning that there was an invisible barrier between the actors and the audience.

Brecht led the way in changing this approach, making sure that the audience were aware that they were watching a play and not real life. Brecht's style influenced the 'house style' of British theatres like the Theatre Workshop.

In what ways is *A Taste of Honey* Brechtian?

Brecht used songs and music in his plays, as Delaney does. The script specifies that there is a jazz trio. However, the music, unlike in most Brecht plays, is incidental and not essential to the plot. When Jimmie 'sings to the audience', the script does not say what he sings. Music is used as a bridge between scenes. When characters enter they are often described as 'dancing' onto the set. This helps to give the play an atmosphere more like that of a variety show or music hall performance, reflecting Littlewood's ideas about **'popular theatre'**.

Characters occasionally break the 'fourth wall' by addressing the audience directly, even asking questions. It is mostly Helen who does this.

Key Quotations to Learn

He waves good-bye, turns and sings to the audience and goes. HELEN *dances on to the music …* (Act 1 Scene 2)

GEOF *dances in with* **props** *for the next scene, which in reality would be a month or two later.* (Act 2 Scene 1)

JO *watches her go, leaning against the doorpost. Then she looks round the room, smiling a little to herself – she remembers* GEOF. (Act 2 Scene 2)

Summary

- There is one set that stays the same throughout.
- The stage directions reflect the style of the original production.
- Aspects of the play's style and staging can be described as Brechtian.
- Music is used in a way that reflects the Theatre Workshop's ideas about popular theatre.

Questions

QUICK TEST
1. Should you quote and comment on stage directions?
2. Which two locations are shown on the stage?
3. How do the actors 'break the fourth wall'?
4. Are directors, actors and designers obliged to use the stage directions printed in the script?

EXAM PRACTICE
Using at least one of the 'Key Quotations to Learn', write a paragraph explaining how the original staging helps to involve the audience in the story of *A Taste of Honey*.

Salford in the 1950s

You must be able to: understand how the place and time in which it is set influence the play.

When and where is *A Taste of Honey* set?

A note at the beginning of the first edition of the play says that it is set in Salford but the opening stage direction refers to a flat in Manchester and later Jo refers to a 'Manchester maisonette'. Salford and Manchester are separate cities but are very close together so people quite often refer to Manchester, the bigger city, when talking about Salford.

The play is set at the time it was written, 1958.

What was the area like in the 1950s?

Salford and Manchester, like many other towns in northern England, had expanded and become densely populated industrial towns in the nineteenth century. Cotton mills built during the **Industrial Revolution** were a source of great wealth for the owners and low-paid employment for workers who migrated from the countryside. Towards the end of the nineteenth century, the Manchester Ship Canal was built to link east Lancashire to Liverpool and the sea, and docks were built in Salford.

In the early twentieth century, there were many slums in Salford. The housing situation was made worse when the city was bombed in the Second World War. After the war, the council embarked on a house-building programme, providing houses for families like the Delaneys.

Education throughout the country was selective – children took the 'eleven plus' exam and were sent to grammar schools if they passed, and secondary moderns if they failed. Unemployment was low and there was plenty of low-paid work in factories, offices and shops available to girls and boys when they left school. They could leave school from the age of 15.

How is life in the area portrayed in the play?

The housing shortage is reflected in Jo and Helen's living conditions. Many people lived in cramped privately rented flats or rooms in old houses, usually with shared bathrooms and toilets. Helen would not have been unusual in moving from flat to flat, possibly without paying the rent (known as 'flitting' or 'doing a flit'). This situation was not unique to Salford at the time but was common in cities and towns throughout the country.

The employment situation is reflected in the ease with which Jo gets a variety of different jobs.

Delaney gives a sense of the industrial landscape of 1950s Salford through references to the canal and docks, the gas works, **tenements**, the cemetery and the slaughterhouse. These all suggest a location very close to Salford Docks (now the Salford Quays development). The sounds of children playing in the street, a fairground and a tugboat are heard.

A few specific places are mentioned. Helen refers to a 'a tatty little pub down Whit Lane'. Later, reminiscing about her childhood, she refers to a place called Shining Clough, in the High Peak of Derbyshire, providing a contrast with the play's urban setting. Geof goes to art school, probably the Manchester School of Art.

Summary

- The play is set in Salford, an industrial city in Lancashire, in the late 1950s.
- The play reflects the city's housing problems after the war.
- Children could leave school at 15 and jobs were easy to get.
- References are made to features of Salford's urban landscape, helping to create a sense of place.

Questions

QUICK TEST
1. What was the main industry in Salford in the nineteenth and early twentieth centuries?
2. What major problem was the city left with after the Second World War?
3. Which waterway connects Salford Docks to the sea?
4. Name three places that help give a sense of the city's landscape.

EXAM PRACTICE

Helen: Everything in it's falling apart, it's true, and we've no heating – but there's a lovely view of the gasworks, we share a bathroom with the community and this wallpaper's contemporary. (Act 1 Scene 1)

Relating your ideas to the context of time and place, write a paragraph analysing how Delaney establishes the setting and Jo and Helen's situation in this quotation.

Sex and Marriage

You must be able to: understand attitudes to sex and marriage in the 1950s and how they are reflected in the play.

How did attitudes to sex differ in the 1950s from now?

It is important not to assume that everyone in the 1950s shared the same social attitudes, just as not everyone today shares the same attitudes and opinions.

However, it is fair to say that in the 1950s the conventional view was that sex outside marriage was immoral, teenage pregnancy was undesirable and that children should be brought up by a mother and father who were married to each other.

How does *A Taste of Honey* reflect these attitudes?

Delaney chose to write about characters who do not always follow these conventions.

Helen has been married but Jo was born as the result of an affair and since then they have been what is now known as a 'single-parent family' (but was not then, when it was less common). Jo indicates that Helen has had a lot of boyfriends and that she has taken money in exchange for sex. She also **implies** that Helen has had abortions. Audiences might be shocked by this, perhaps more at the time of writing than now, but might also wonder if Jo is telling the truth.

Jo gets involved in a sexual relationship as soon as she leaves school. It is not clear how old she is but she is probably 16 or 17 (she tells the Boy she is nearly 18). She immediately becomes pregnant. The most common options taken by unmarried pregnant women at the time were marriage to the father or adoption (usually formally but sometimes informally within the family). Abortion, although illegal at the time, is mentioned but Jo rejects the idea. It was not unknown for single women to bring up their children alone (something Delaney herself did later in life) but **social stigma** and financial difficulty made it unusual.

Peter has clearly had a lot of girlfriends and Jo suggests that he might be married to someone else when he is courting Helen. This would be unacceptable to most people both then and now. Jo makes light of it and it does not seem to be true. However, he and Helen have not been married long before he has an affair.

In *A Taste of Honey*, there is an awareness of the accepted conventions of the time and some desire to be 'respectable' and abide by them. Peter and Helen marry, and Jo and Jimmie get engaged. Geof offers to marry Jo and be a father to the baby. The characters do not expressly criticise these **norms** or set out to rebel against them. However, they are unwilling or unable to live by them and there is a sense that, while they might sometimes aspire to society's conventions, they are generally tolerant of their own and others' failure to adhere to them.

Delaney's characters' attitudes to sex and marriage were not often portrayed on the stage or in the media at the time. The play reveals that not everyone shared the same morality or lived according to the same rules in 1950s Britain – one of the things that made it controversial when it was first staged.

Summary

- At the time the play is set, sex before marriage was generally frowned on and most people believed that children should be brought up by two married parents.
- The most common options for single pregnant women were marriage and adoption.
- Delaney's characters acknowledge these conventions and sometimes aspire to them.
- None of them, however, stick to them, showing a different side of 1950s Britain.

Questions

QUICK TEST
1. What were the two most common options for pregnant single women in the 1950s?
2. Do Delaney's characters follow the sexual conventions of the time?
3. How do Helen, Peter, Jo and Geof all show a desire to follow convention?
4. What did the play show audiences about 1950s sexual morality?

EXAM PRACTICE
Relating your ideas to historical context, write a paragraph exploring how Delaney conveys her characters' feelings about marriage.

Race and Sexuality

You must be able to: understand attitudes to race and sexuality in the 1950s and how they are reflected in the play.

How did attitudes to race differ in the 1950s from now?

In the 1950s, Britain was much less ethnically diverse than it is today. Despite increasing immigration from the West Indies and Asia after the Second World War, many people in Britain would have had very little contact with non-white people.

Until the Race Relations Act of 1965 was passed, it was not illegal to discriminate against people because of their race or colour. Opinions and language that are generally considered racially offensive today were widespread and more socially acceptable.

How does *A Taste of Honey* reflect these attitudes?

When the play first appeared, Delaney was praised for showing a relationship between people of different races and not making an 'issue' out of it. However, both Jo and Jimmie show that they are conscious that it could be an issue for others, Jimmie by suggesting that Jo might not want to be seen with him and Jo by her interest in his background. Jo's **fantasy** about him being an African prince, while **stereotypical**, suggests his race intrigues and attracts her. He plays on this with his reference to *Othello*.

Helen's reaction to finding out that the baby 'might be black' suggests that this is more of a concern to her than the fact that Jo is not married. However, she makes a joke out of it.

How did attitudes to sexuality differ in the 1950s from now?

Sexual acts between men were illegal in Britain until 1967. Most people in Britain did not approve of homosexuality. Offensive language and violence aimed at gay people were more common than they are today. Homosexuality tended to be seen as either a social and psychological problem or a subject of comedy. Few people were openly gay.

How does *A Taste of Honey* reflect these attitudes?

Delaney has been praised for portraying Geof in an unsensational and largely non-stereotypical way – although some might see his interest in **traditionally** female domestic chores such as sewing and even the fact that he is an art student as somewhat stereotypical. Others would call this realistic, people in the arts perhaps being more likely than those in other areas to be open about their sexuality.

As with race, sexuality is not treated as a 'problem'. Nevertheless, Helen's and Peter's use of **phrases** such as 'fruitcake parcel' and 'bloody little pansy' to insult Geof reflect common perceptions. Although he does not confirm it, Jo suspects Geof has been thrown out of his flat because of his sexuality. She is curious but accepting. Geof himself is not entirely comfortable with his sexuality, refusing to discuss it with Jo and showing a desire to conform to prevailing sexual norms when he kisses Jo and asks her to marry him.

Summary

- British society was less racially diverse in the 1950s and discrimination on racial grounds was not illegal.
- Race is not often referred to in the play but characters are aware of racial **prejudice**.
- Sexual acts between men were illegal until 1967.
- Helen's and Peter's attitudes reflect the attitudes of society to homosexuality.

Questions

QUICK TEST
1. When was the Race Relations Act, banning discrimination, passed?
2. To which Shakespeare play does Jimmie refer?
3. What is Jo's reaction to Geof's homosexuality?
4. Which two characters insult Geof because of his sexuality?

EXAM PRACTICE
'Did your ancestors come from Africa?' (Act 1 Scene 2)

Relating your ideas to the historical context, write a paragraph explaining Jo's feelings about Jimmie's race.

You must be able to: analyse how Jo is presented in Act 1.

Who is Jo?

Jo lives with her divorced mother, Helen. Her father was not the man Helen was married to and Helen has brought her up alone. At the beginning of the play, she is still at school.

What is her function in the play?

She is the play's **protagonist**. She is rarely off stage and the play focuses on what happens to her over a period of just under a year.

What is her character and how does she reveal it?

She is a complex character, full of contradictions.

It is clear from the beginning that Jo, although dependent on her mother, has a mind of her own and she does not hesitate to express her opinions. She often does this in a humorous way and it is not always clear whether she is being serious.

In some ways, Jo is independent and mature. She speaks to her mother as an equal and discusses 'adult' subjects. She can be quite cynical. However, she is also naive, as shown by her curiosity about the Boy and her trust in him. This child-like quality is also shown in her fear of the dark.

She is keen to leave school. She is unsettled and restless. Although she claims to know what she wants, she has no aims or ambitions beyond leaving school and getting a job.

She shows a creative side through her drawings and a desire for beauty in her attempts to make the flat more cheerful.

She shows a romantic side in her scene with the Boy and she is curious about sex. She flirts with Peter. Her interactions with Peter and Helen also show that she can be temperamental and childish.

She is unconventional and lacking in prejudice.

How do other characters react to Jo?

Her 'love–hate' relationship with Helen is central to the play. It is dealt with in more detail on pages 40 to 41.

Peter does not know what to make of her. She is hostile towards him, **interrogates** him about his past and flirts with him. Helen thinks she is jealous.

With the Boy, she is more serious and expresses her feelings for him. He seems to feel the same way but subsequent events might make the audience ask whether his feelings are genuine. Jo herself says that she knows he won't return.

Key Quotations to Learn

Helen: It's very good. Did you show them this at school?
Jo: I'm never at one school long enough to show them anything.
Helen: That's my fault, I suppose. (Act 1 Scene 1)

Jo: Do I bother you, Mister Smith, or must I wait till we're alone for an answer?
Peter: Can't you keep her under control? (Act 1 Scene 2)

Jo: I just know it. That's all. But I don't care. Stay with me now, it's enough, it's all I want, and if you do come back I'll still be here. (Act 1 Scene 2)

Summary

- Jo is the play's protagonist.
- She is mature in some ways but child-like in others.
- She has a forthright manner but it is not always clear whether she is being serious.
- She is cynical, romantic, creative, restless and unprejudiced.

Sample Analysis

Jo's first line in the play is 'And I don't like it.' Immediately the audience sees the tension between mother and daughter, Jo's forthright manner and her negativity. This negativity is reinforced by the use of the phrase 'old ruin' to describe the flat and her complaints that she's 'cold' and her shoes 'let in water'. The audience might feel sympathy for Jo but might also be surprised, or even shocked, by the way she speaks to Helen, blaming her for the situation ('You can afford something better …') and implying that she makes money from sex in her reference to 'immoral earnings'.

Questions

QUICK TEST
1. With whom does Jo have a 'love–hate' relationship?
2. How is Jo's creativity shown?
3. With which character does Jo reveal her romantic side?

EXAM PRACTICE
Using at least one of the 'Key Quotations to Learn', write a paragraph explaining how Delaney presents Jo in Act 1.

You must be able to: analyse how Jo is presented in Act 2.

How does Jo change in Act 2?

Jo is pregnant. Her focus and that of the play are on her pregnancy and what the future will hold for her and her baby. Her character does not change dramatically but her insecurity and moodiness increase.

How does she show her character through her actions?

At the start of Scene 1, Jo does not want Geof to put the lights on because of the state of the flat. It is clear that she has not been looking after herself or the flat.

She shows kindness by inviting Geof to stay but she upsets him with her curiosity about his sexuality. However, she quickly regrets hurting his feelings.

She gives the impression of not caring about the future or her baby. Her gloomy thoughts make Geof think that she is depressed.

She settles down a bit after Geof has moved in but remains moody and argumentative. She also flirts with him but turns on him when he responds.

When Helen arrives, Jo becomes angry and asserts her independence by refusing her help.

In Act 2 Scene 2, although she still makes jokes, her mood is dark again. She reacts violently to the doll that Geof has bought her. She becomes reflective, talking about Jimmie as 'a dream I had'. She says that she doesn't want any man, having earlier said she did not want to marry. This contrasts with Act 1 when she wanted to get married.

When Helen returns, Jo is resentful at first but, after Geof has gone, she accepts her help.

How do other characters react to Jo in Act 2?

Geof is sympathetic to her and cares for her. He is able to calm her down and talk seriously to her. Their shared life in the flat contrasts with her life with Helen in Act 1.

Helen wants to help Jo but is very critical and draws a hostile reaction. Peter is now very hostile towards her.

Is she a strong character?

Some critics have argued that Jo is a strong character, overcoming inequality to make her own life. She rejects marriage and is willing to bring up her baby alone (although the open ending means that it is not certain that she will do this).

However, while she asserts her independence and stands up for herself, this might just be bluster, hiding her insecurity. She can be quite a passive character, reacting to events and other people rather than making decisions and taking control of events.

Key Quotations to Learn

Geof: You're feeling a bit depressed, Jo.
Jo: I'm feeling nothing. (Act 2 Scene 1)

Jo: I told you to keep out of my affairs, Geoffrey. I'm not having anybody running my life for me. (Act 2 Scene 1)

Jo: … Do you know, for the first time in my life I feel really important. I feel as though I could take care of the whole world … (Act 2 Scene 2)

Summary

- In the second act, Jo is pregnant.
- She has been neglecting herself but Geof takes care of her.
- Her mood changes a lot: sometimes depressed, sometimes angry, sometimes light-hearted.
- She strongly asserts her independence but lets others make decisions for her.

Sample Analysis

When Jo tells Geof about her father, she romanticises what Helen told her in Act 1. She says that he was Irish and that he was the 'village idiot', whereas Helen called him 'a bit stupid' and 'a bit retarded'. She never mentioned a connection with Ireland or 'a frolic in a hayloft'. Jo's version of events is made up of literary cliches, such as saying her father lived in 'a twilight land', a reference to the 'Celtic Twilight' of Irish literature. The audience does not know whether Jo believes her own story or why she tells it to Geof in this way – to amuse him, to gain sympathy, to hide her real concerns or a combination of all of these?

Questions

QUICK TEST
1. Who is living with Jo during Act 2?
2. What does Geof give Jo that makes her angry?
3. How has Jo's attitude to marriage changed since Act 1?
4. How does her attitude to Helen change between Act 2 Scene 1 and the end of the play?

EXAM PRACTICE
Using at least one of the 'Key Quotations to Learn', write a paragraph explaining how Delaney presents Jo in Act 2.

You must be able to: analyse how Helen is presented in the play.

Who is Helen?

Helen is Jo's mother. She is divorced and aged about 40. She has had a lot of boyfriends.

What is her function in the play?

Helen can be seen as the play's **antagonist**, the character who opposes the protagonist, Jo.

What is her character?

She is self-centred, pleasure-seeking, unreliable, argumentative, funny and **fatalistic**.

How does she show her character through her actions?

Helen has made the decision to move without thinking about Jo, although she acknowledges that it will be awkward for her. Her selfishness is shown when she leaves with Peter and it is revealed that it is not the first time that she has left Jo alone when going off with men.

She does not have much money but says she is 'careful' with what she has. She drinks whisky and enjoys going to pubs and cinemas with men.

There is a suggestion that she might take money for sex, as she is initially described as a 'semi-whore' and Jo refers to her 'immoral earnings', but this could just mean that she is happy to accept presents and treats from men. She is, however, clearly sexually active and Jo speaks of being turned out of the bed so Helen can sleep with men.

She shows a desire for a better, more comfortable and happier life. She reminisces about singing in pubs, saying she could have been a singer. She is keen to marry Peter and move to a nice house with him.

She argues constantly with Jo, shouting at her and threatening her with violence, but changes her mood quickly. Like Jo, she is humorous and makes a joke out of most things.

At the end of the play, she displays a caring side as she moves back in with Jo. However, it is not clear how much this is due to her feelings for Jo and how much it is because she has left Peter and needs somewhere to live.

She is not really a strong character. She lives from day to day and is dependent on men. However, she is resilient, bouncing back from difficult situations and (usually cheerfully) getting on with life.

How do other characters react to Helen?

Jo is critical of her behaviour. She does not respect her but, towards the end of the play, misses her.

Peter sees her as attractive and fun. He seems genuine in wanting to marry her but soon has an affair with another woman.

Geof does not like her or her behaviour but thinks she should be with Jo.

Key Quotations to Learn

Jo: You always have to rush off into things. You never think. (Act 1 Scene 1)

Helen: I've done my share of suffering if I never do any more. (Act 1 Scene 2)

Helen: He's gone off with his bit of crumpet. Still, it was good while it lasted. (Act 2 Scene 2)

Summary

- Helen is Jo's mother and her antagonist.
- She is self-centred and pleasure-seeking.
- She is argumentative but funny.
- She is not a very strong character but she is resilient.

Sample Analysis

Helen's attitude to Jo is inconsistent: at times she talks to her as an adult, sometimes she treats her like a naughty child. When Jo surmises (accurately) that she is 'running away from somebody', Helen shuts her down with 'You're asking for a bloody good hiding', showing her strength of feeling by adding the mild swear word 'bloody' to the **dialect** phrase 'good hiding'. She addresses her daughter as 'lady', a form of address used sarcastically – and sometimes aggressively – in Lancashire during **admonishments** or arguments.

Questions

QUICK TEST
1. Where has Helen worked in the past?
2. How does she describe her attitude to money?
3. Why does she leave Jo alone in the flat?
4. Give two reasons for Helen moving back in with Jo.

EXAM PRACTICE
Using at least one of the 'Key Quotations to Learn', write a paragraph explaining how Delaney presents Helen's attitude to life.

You must be able to: analyse how Peter is presented in the play.

Who is Peter?

Peter is Helen's boyfriend, later husband.

What is his function in the play?

His relationship with Helen creates tension between her and Jo. Their marriage marks the end of Act 1 and means that Jo is left alone.

What is his character?

For most audiences, he is the least sympathetic character in the play.

He is a **philanderer** and a drinker. He makes crude jokes and uses sexual **innuendo**. He has no patience with Jo and is offensive to Geof.

He is unreliable. According to the stage directions, he is '*a brash car salesman*'. His occupation is stereotypical shorthand for being flashy and dishonest. He is well-off compared with Helen and Jo, and is generous to Helen.

His war service and his injury might gain him some sympathy.

How does he show his character through his actions?

In Act 1 Scene 1, he has tracked Helen down and wants her back. She is reluctant at first but he talks her round with flattery and an offer of marriage.

When he returns in Act 1 Scene 2, he is '*looking uncomfortable*'. He and Helen seem happy together so it must be Jo who makes him feel uncomfortable. She soon begins to irritate him and even attacks him physically.

His photographs lead Jo to suggest he has had 'thousands of girlfriends', which he does not deny but treats as a joke. She later asks if he is married. He denies it. He replies to Jo's questions about his eye patch and war service but ends the discussion by joking.

By Act 2 he is married to Helen. He arrives at the flat drunk, using coarse language and insulting Geof, Jo and Helen, as well as the flat and the area. He is annoyed when Helen invites Jo to come and live with them.

How do other characters react to Peter?

Jo does not like him, partly just because he is Helen's boyfriend, and they become increasingly hostile to each other. She interrogates him, flirts with him and provokes him.

It is not clear whether Helen loves him, but she enjoys his company and likes him spending money on her. By Act 2 Scene 2 the relationship is breaking down.

Key Quotations to Learn

Peter: Helen, you don't seem to realize what an opportunity I'm giving you. The world is littered with women I've rejected … (Act 1 Scene 1)

Jo: What are you marrying him for?
Helen: He's got a wallet full of reasons. (Act 1 Scene 2)

Peter: … I dragged you out of the gutter once. If you want to go back there it's all the same to me. (Act 2 Scene 1)

Summary

- Peter is Helen's boyfriend and later husband.
- He is a stereotypical flashy car salesman.
- In the second act, when drunk, he is offensive and aggressive.
- Jo dislikes him and provokes him.

Sample Analysis

In Act 1 Scene 2, Peter gives chocolates to Jo. This suggests that he wants to get on with her. At first, she reacts with a sharp but humorous exclamation, 'Buying my silence, hey!' She soon starts to irritate him by the way she eats the chocolates and he tells her off with a negative command: 'Don't sit there guzzling all those chocolates at once.' Her reaction is surprising and violent as the stage direction says *'She throws the lid at him'* which makes him swear ('What the hell …'). He uses **imperatives** ('sit down and behave yourself') and a mild insult ('you little snip') to try to control her but she reacts more violently, attacking him *'half-laughing, half-crying'* and telling him to 'leave my mother alone'. This suggests that she is protective of Helen and frightened of losing her to Peter.

Questions

QUICK TEST
1. Why does Peter wear an eye patch?
2. What do the pictures in his wallet tell Jo?
3. How does he behave towards Helen in Act 2 Scene 2?

EXAM PRACTICE
Using at least one of the 'Key Quotations to Learn', write a paragraph explaining how Delaney presents Peter's relationship with Helen.

The Boy (Jimmie)

You must be able to: analyse how the Boy is presented in the play.

Who is the Boy?

The stage directions refer to him as Jo's '*boyfriend, a coloured naval rating*'. He is a former nurse who is doing **National Service** in the Royal Navy.

What is his function in the play?

The fact that he is not given a name in the first act suggests that his role as Jo's boyfriend and the father of her child is his sole function. The fact that his ethnicity is specified indicates that this might be an issue for other characters and/or audiences.

What is his character?

He seems to be gentle, caring, charming, well-educated (he quotes Shakespeare) and funny but proves unreliable.

How does he show his character through his actions?

Although he is 22, he is called 'the Boy' in the text. Jo talks about 'little boys' when he empties his pockets, suggesting immaturity.

He tells her he loves her and looks after her when she is upset after Helen leaves.

He is open about wanting to have sex with Jo but respects her wishes. He asks her to marry him, gives her a (cheap) ring and promises to return. He does not return.

How do other characters react to the Boy?

Jo is the only other character seen with the Boy. She enjoys his company and says that she loves him. She is pleased to see him after Helen leaves and invites him to stay.

She is curious about his background and, despite him telling her he is from Cardiff, fantasises about him being an African prince before telling Geof the truth and revealing his real name, Jimmie.

Although she agrees to marry him when he returns, she says that she does not expect him to come back.

How might audiences react to him?

When the play was first produced, it was unusual to see inter-racial relationships on stage so some audience members may have been shocked or disapproving.

Jo says jokingly that he is 'only after one thing' despite him saying that he loves her. As he is older and more experienced than her, audiences might think that he has taken advantage of Jo and is indeed 'only after one thing'. They might also suspect that he is not as committed to the relationship as he claims when he chooses a drink with 'the lads' over meeting Jo.

Key Quotations to Learn

Boy: Afraid someone'll see us?
Jo: I don't care. (Act 1 Scene 2)

Boy: I didn't take advantage. I had scruples. (Act 1 Scene 2)

Boy: I've got dishonourable intentions.
Jo: I'm so glad. (Act 1 Scene 2)

Summary

- Jo's boyfriend is not given a name until he is no longer in the play.
- He is a black sailor, formerly a nurse, from Cardiff.
- He is charming and appears to love and care for Jo.
- He does not return in Act 2.

Sample Analysis

Towards the end of Act 1, the Boy quotes from Shakespeare's *Othello.* The reference to 'the gross clasps of the lascivious Moor' is lost on Jo but it makes the audience think about the Boy's race. Othello is also older and more experienced than Desdemona and their marriage is opposed by her father. Audiences might recall the tragic ending of *Othello*, when he kills Desdemona because of jealousy and his passion for her, and wonder how Jo and the Boy's relationship will develop. However, the Boy ends his relationship with Jo in a much more **prosaic** way: he deserts her with no explanation. *A Taste of Honey* is not a tragic love story.

Questions

QUICK TEST
1. Why is the Boy in the Navy?
2. What does he buy for Jo?
3. What two promises does he make to Jo?
4. What does Jo tell Geof about the Boy before she tells the truth?

EXAM PRACTICE
Using at least one of the 'Key Quotations to Learn', write a paragraph explaining how Delaney presents the Boy.

You must be able to: analyse how Geof is presented in the play.

Who is Geof?

Geof is an art student who befriends Jo and moves into her flat. He is gay.

What is his function in the play?

Geof only appears in Act 2. He acts as a **confidant** to Jo and replaces both Helen and the Boy in her life in different ways.

What is his character?

He is caring, sensitive and practical.

How does he show his character through his actions?

As soon as he arrives in the flat, he realises that Jo is not looking after herself. He takes responsibility for shopping, cleaning, paying the rent and even planning for the baby.

He is angry when Jo brings up his sexuality by saying she has 'always wanted to know about people like you'; he thinks she is making fun of him. The row is short lived, as are other disagreements between them.

He is critical of Jo's drawings, casting an expert eye over them and calling them **'sentimental'**. His honest response contrasts with Helen's earlier reaction to them.

During the remainder of Act 2, he gives both emotional and practical support to Jo. He gets her a new job, makes clothes for the baby, gets a book about babies and buys a cot. Although Jo sometimes gets annoyed or makes sarcastic comments, he is patient with her. He tells Helen that Jo has asked him to be with her at the birth.

He kisses Jo and says that he wants to marry her, showing that he wants to be part of a conventional family. He says that he could not live without her. Emotionally, he has become as dependent on her as she has on him.

When he gets Helen to visit and later leaves at her request, he puts Jo and the baby before himself, showing a selflessness that contrasts with the selfishness of Helen, Peter, the Boy and even Jo.

How do other characters react to Geof?

At the beginning of Act 2, Jo and Geof are described as 'playing together', suggesting an innocent child-like friendship. His sexuality interests her and, although they flirt, their relationship is **platonic**. She says he is like her 'big sister'.

Helen resents him, perhaps because he has taken her place, insults him with **derogatory** comments about his sexuality and effectively throws him out.

Peter, who is drunk when they meet, is even more offensive than Helen and tells Jo not to bring him with her if she moves in with them.

Key Quotations to Learn

Geof: I can't stand people who laugh at other people. They'd get a bigger laugh if they laughed at themselves. (Act 2 Scene 1)

Geof: How are you going to manage then?
Jo: There's no need for you to worry about it.
Geof: Somebody's got to. Anyway, I like you. (Act 2 Scene 1)

Jo: I always want to have you with me because I know you'll never ask anything from me. (Act 2 Scene 2)

Summary

- Geof is artistic and sensitive but practical.
- Although he flirts with and kisses Jo, their relationship is platonic.
- He supports Jo in emotional and practical ways.
- He acts selflessly when he leaves Jo with Helen.

Sample Analysis

In Act 2, after kissing Jo, Geof says 'I'd sooner be dead than away from you', which seems **hyperbolic**, even **melodramatic**, and leaves Jo confused. When he insists that he means what he has said and she asks him why, he reveals that before he met her 'I didn't care whether I lived or died'. This might remind the audience of his earlier suggestion that Jo was depressed. His diagnosis of her mental state might be based on his own experience of depression. His honest confession surprises Jo and she does not react with her usual sarcastic humour but ends the conversation by lying down.

Questions

QUICK TEST
1. What does Geof think of Jo's drawings?
2. Give three ways in which he offers practical support to Jo.
3. Who does he tell about Jo's pregnancy in an effort to help her?

EXAM PRACTICE
Using at least one of the 'Key Quotations to Learn', write a paragraph explaining how Delaney presents Geof's relationship with Jo.

Pregnancy and Motherhood

You must be able to: understand and analyse how the themes of pregnancy and motherhood are explored in the play.

How does Jo feel about her pregnancy and becoming a mother?

Because Jo is already several months pregnant at the beginning of Act 2 we do not know what her initial feelings about pregnancy were. Now she seems to just accept the situation.

She rejects the idea of abortion, calling it 'terrible'. However, she has violent thoughts about the baby, shown in her reaction to the doll. She also likens breast-feeding to being eaten by an animal, calling it 'cannibalistic' and saying she hates motherhood. Geof suggests that she is nervous and frightened about the idea of giving birth.

She does not respond to Geof's suggestion that she gives the baby up for adoption and at no point in the play says whether or not she intends to keep the baby after it is born.

How do other characters react to Jo's pregnancy?

As far as we know, Jimmie is unaware of the pregnancy.

Geof is supportive. Until Helen returns, he is planning to be present at the birth and likes the idea of being a father to the baby.

At first, Helen is angry about Jo getting pregnant but she later offers to help. She wants to buy things for the baby and be at the birth but the audience might wonder how serious she is.

Peter makes a joke of it and insults Jo.

What is Helen's attitude to being a mother?

Helen has not been an attentive mother to Jo, often leaving her alone and not taking her feelings or needs into account, for example when moving house.

Helen says that she does not believe mothers have responsibility for their children.

She does, however, show some maternal feelings when, at Geof's request, she visits Jo and offers her a home and later when she reassures Jo about her contractions.

She finds the idea of Geof being with Jo at the birth 'disgusting', believing that men should have nothing to do with birth. This was a common view at the time the play was written. Few men attended the births of their children.

Key Quotations to Learn

Geof: You can get rid of babies before they're born, you know.
Jo: I know, but I think that's terrible. (Act 2 Scene 1)

Jo: Shut up! I'm not planning big plans for this baby, or dreaming big dreams. You know what happens when you do things like that. The baby'll be born dead or daft! (Act 2 Scene 1)

Geof: She said she wanted me with her when she had it because she said she wouldn't be frightened if I was with her.
Helen: How disgusting! (Act 2 Scene 2)

Summary

- Jo has mixed feelings about pregnancy and the baby but wants to have it.
- She says she does not want to make plans but lets Geof make plans for her.
- When she is angry and upset, she says she will kill the baby.
- At times she seems confident about the future but at other times she is nervous.

Sample Analysis

Reacting to Jo's pregnancy, Helen says that 'bearing a child doesn't place one under an obligation to it'. While she is referring to her own role as Jo's mother, Helen's statement, made in quite formal, impersonal language, using the pronoun 'one', could be taken as an indication to Jo that she is not expected to look after her baby. Helen uses this unconventional and to many people shocking idea, which is challenged by Geof, to justify her neglect of and indifference to Jo in the past. She is defensive but defiant as she tells Geof not to 'stand there looking as if it's my fault'. She refuses to take responsibility for how her child's life has turned out.

Questions

QUICK TEST
1. How does Helen initially react to Jo's pregnancy?
2. Why does Jo say she is not making plans for the baby?
3. Which male character supports Jo in her pregnancy?

EXAM PRACTICE
Using at least one of the 'Key Quotations to Learn', write a paragraph explaining how Delaney presents Jo's feelings about pregnancy.

Mother–Daughter Relationships

You must be able to: understand the relationship between Jo and Helen and its importance in the play.

Why is this relationship important?

The relationship between Jo and her mother Helen is central to the play. They are the play's protagonist and antagonist.

What is the nature of their relationship?

They live together and appear to have no other family or friends. Helen has brought up Jo as a single parent. Jo has never known her biological father and Helen left her husband – who was not Jo's father – when Jo was a baby.

They do not have a conventional parent–child relationship. Jo calls Helen by her first name and in some ways Helen treats her as an adult. Jo has been left to fend for herself from an early age and Helen's attempts to act like a more conventional mother – for example, giving advice on relationships or praising her art – are ignored or rejected. At other times, however, Jo criticises Helen for not acting like a mother.

They can be seen as **'sparring partners'**. It can be hard to tell whether they are being serious as their insults and accusations are often humorous. Helen claims they enjoy fighting.

Helen accuses Jo of being jealous of her. Audiences might see Jo's reaction to Peter as a desire for attention and maternal love.

Their relationship has been described as a 'love–hate' relationship.

Do they show love for each other?

Neither of them expresses love or affection openly.

There are some close, almost affectionate moments between them, such as when Jo tells Helen about her boyfriend. They might seem more like friends or sisters at these times.

Jo admits to Geof that she misses Helen.

When Helen returns, she says she – as a mother – is needed 'at a time like this'. She is trying to play a traditional mother's role but in doing so she ignores or criticises Jo's wishes.

The final scene between them is affectionate and touching but the audience might doubt Helen's sincerity and, when she exits, whether she will be there for Jo.

The mother–daughter relationship is the only enduring relationship in the play but it is fragile.

Key Quotations to Learn

Jo: … You've never cared much before about what I was doing or what I was trying to do or the difference between them.
Helen: I know, I'm a cruel, wicked woman. (Act 1 Scene 1)

Geof: (*yelling*) Will you stop shouting, you two?
Helen: We enjoy it. (Act 2 Scene 1)

Helen: After all, I am …
Jo: After all you are my mother! You're a bit late remembering that, aren't you? (Act 2 Scene 1)

Summary

- The relationship between mother and daughter is a central theme of the play.
- Helen and Jo's relationship is not a traditional or conventional parent–child relationship.
- It is often seen as a 'love–hate' relationship.
- It is the only relationship in the play that endures.

Sample Analysis

In a rare serious and sentimental moment, Jo tells Geof about how she used to try to hold Helen's hand. She downplays Helen's rejection by using the childish **adjective** 'silly' to describe it. She says that Helen had 'so much love for everyone else, but none for me', showing that despite her often cynical response to Helen and her love life, she feels the rejection deeply. It may be this cynicism that makes Geof say she will 'turn out exactly like her' and that in 'some ways' she is already like Helen. His point is underlined when Jo '*pushes his hand away*', an ambiguous gesture as the stage direction does not say whether it is done humorously or instinctively. Either way, it recreates Helen's rejection of her own love.

Questions

QUICK TEST
1. Give an example of a way in which Helen tries to show an interest in Jo in Act 1.
2. Does Jo think Helen has been a good mother?
3. What reason does Helen give for returning at the end of the play?

EXAM PRACTICE
Using at least one of the 'Key Quotations to Learn', write a paragraph analysing how Delaney presents Jo's relationship with Helen.

Love and Sex

You must be able to: analyse how ideas about love and sex are presented in the play.

How is Jo's relationship with the Boy presented?

The Boy is introduced in an intimate scene that takes place in a small area of the set representing the street outside the flat.

Both characters talk of being in love. The Boy says he has not pressed Jo into having sex, respecting her wishes. He buys her a ring and asks her to marry him.

His reference to *Othello* suggests their love is stronger because of the potential difficulties posed by his race. Their relationship is secret. They meet in darkness and Jo hides the ring.

Despite the tenderness that the Boy shows towards Jo and his promises, Jo says that she knows he will not return. She later talks of the relationship as a 'dream'.

Jo says that she'd never been 'familiar' with love, implying that she does not feel loved by her mother.

Audiences might take a cynical view of the Boy's declarations of love and think he has taken advantage of Jo, particularly given the difference in their ages.

How is Helen and Peter's relationship presented?

In contrast, Helen and Peter's relationship is presented as being primarily about sex. She might be attracted to his money more than to him.

There are elements of a traditional romantic 'courtship', however. Peter buys flowers for Helen, takes her out and, in contrast to Jimmie, actually marries her. Peter pursues Helen and seems to need her more than she needs him.

It is a tempestuous on–off relationship and Helen does not appear upset when it ends.

How is Jo's relationship with Geof presented?

Although his sexuality is made clear soon after his first entrance, Geof kisses Jo and seems to want a sexual relationship with her. When she rejects this, he settles for a platonic relationship. However, he expresses his feelings for Jo in passionate, romantic terms and says he cannot live without her.

The relationship contrasts with Jo's relationship with the Boy and Helen's relationship with Peter.

How is sex seen in *A Taste of Honey*?

None of the characters talk about sex in moral terms. Even when Helen discovers Jo is pregnant she condemns her actions as stupid rather than wrong.

Jo's experience puts her off sexual relationships. Her friendship with Geof is presented as an alternative to traditional sexual/romantic relationships.

Key Quotations to Learn

Helen: I always accept the odd diamond ring with pleasure.
Peter: I know it's my money you're after. (Act 1 Scene 1)

Jo: I don't know much about love. I've never been too familiar with it. I suppose I must have loved him ... (Act 2 Scene 1)

Helen: You know what they're calling you round here? A silly little whore!
Jo: Well, they all know where I get it from too. (Act 2 Scene 1)

Summary

- Jo's relationship with the Boy is presented in a traditionally romantic way.
- Audiences might view it more cynically and Jo is unsure about whether she was in love.
- Helen and Peter have a casual attitude to sex but there are romantic elements in their relationship.
- Jo's relationship with Geof can be seen as an alternative to sexual relationships.

Sample Analysis

In Jo's first scene with the Boy, her youth is constantly referred to. The fact she is on her way home from school, probably in uniform, and he is carrying her books creates an **image** of youthful romance. Both of them refer to Jo as a 'girl' and he calls himself a 'boy' rather than a man. When he empties his pockets, she refers to 'little boys' and finds he has a toy car, implying that he is childish although he is older than her. She refers to her 'schoolgirl complexion' and accuses him, jokingly and flirtatiously, of 'taking advantage of my innocence', and the audience might come to think, in view of later events, that he, unlike her, is far from innocent and has exploited her naivety.

Questions

QUICK TEST
1. What does the Boy give Jo as a **symbol** of his love?
2. How does Peter 'court' Helen?
3. Which relationship can be described as 'platonic'?

EXAM PRACTICE
Using at least one of the 'Key Quotations to Learn', write a paragraph explaining how Delaney presents love in A Taste of Honey.

Outsiders and Misfits

You must be able to: analyse how the idea of being an outsider or a misfit is important in the play.

What is meant by 'outsiders and misfits' and why are they important in *A Taste of Honey*?

Outsiders are people who think of themselves or are thought of by others as not being part of conventional society. Misfits are people who feel they do not fit in. The two concepts overlap.

Delaney was clear that her characters were not meant to be typical of their class or the place in which the play is set. All her characters can be seen as outsiders and/or misfits.

How are the Boy and Geof outsiders?

Both these characters can be seen as outsiders because of social attitudes and prejudice at the time – the Boy because he is black and Geof because he is gay. They are both aware that they are outsiders.

The Boy is quite relaxed about his position in society and does not come across as a misfit – he is aware of prejudice but gets on well with his mates in the Navy and conforms to society's norms by having a job and by joining the Navy for his National Service.

Geof is not happy about being an outsider and shows a desire to fit in by being part of a family, even asking Jo to marry him, in spite of his homosexuality.

Jo is curious about their lives and backgrounds. She might be attracted by their 'difference'.

How are Jo and Helen misfits or outsiders?

Helen and Jo live on the fringes of society. They do not settle down in accommodation, jobs or relationships. Jo feels that she does not fit in at school. Helen's attitude to sex, and the suggestion that she is paid for it, imply that she does not fit in with society's norms.

Jo likes the idea of being different, describing herself and Geof as 'degenerates' and later as 'communists'.

Is Peter a misfit?

Peter has a job, a house and money as well as being a straight white male, so he might seem to be the one character who is not an outsider or misfit. However, his eye patch is a visible sign that he too is 'different'. His drinking and philandering might also place him outside 'respectable' society.

Key Quotations to Learn

Jo: I've had enough of school. Too many different schools and too many different places. (Act 1 Scene 1)

Jo: I don't care where you were born. There's still a bit of jungle in you somewhere. (Act 1 Scene 2)

Jo: We're both beggars. A couple of degenerates.
Geof: The devil's own! (Act 2 Scene 1)

Summary

- The Boy and Geof are outsiders because of, respectively, race and sexuality.
- Jo and Helen are also misfits or outsiders because of their lifestyle.
- Even Peter can be seen as a misfit.
- The play does not include anyone who leads a conventional or respectable life.

Sample Analysis

When the Boy first appears, he is literally an outsider, as the scene takes place outside the flat. His position as a stranger is emphasised by the fact that he is not initially given a name. It is he, not Jo, who brings up his ethnicity, which makes him an outsider, asking 'What will your mother say?' and 'Doesn't she care who her daughter marries?' Jo shows her lack of prejudice by not realising he is thinking about race until he says Helen will 'see a coloured boy', meaning she will judge him by his colour, something Jo denies, saying Helen is not 'prejudiced'. However, Jo is proved wrong at the end of the play by Helen's shocked reaction to her revelation that the baby will be black.

Questions

QUICK TEST
1. In what way is the Boy not a misfit or outsider?
2. What is Jo's attitude to the fact that the Boy and Geof are outsiders?
3. What visual sign shows that Peter is a misfit?

EXAM PRACTICE
Using at least one of the 'Key Quotations to Learn', write a paragraph explaining how Delaney explores the idea of being an outsider or misfit in *A Taste of Honey*.

Poverty

You must be able to: analyse how ideas about poverty are presented in the play.

Who is poor in *A Taste of Honey*?

Jo and Helen do not have much money. They live in poor-quality accommodation and Jo does not have decent shoes or clothes. After Helen leaves, Jo struggles to pay her rent and buy food.

Geof is a student living on a student grant but Jo implies that he is from a better-off, middle-class background when she refers to his 'expensive art school'.

The Boy is not rich. Despite having a secure job, he would not be well paid, and he buys Jo a cheap ring from Woolworths, a shop associated with low prices (although this might also show he is not serious about the relationship).

Peter is comparatively rich with his 'big white house', his car and his ability to buy things like fur coats for Helen.

How is poverty presented in the play?

The descriptions of the flat at the beginning of the play make it clear that Helen and Jo are poor. They only have one bed. They share a bathroom with other tenants. Helen says that 'everything's falling apart'. The area is described as an undesirable place to live.

Jo blames Helen for renting the place and says she can 'afford something better'. Helen responds that she is 'careful' and it is not clear whether she could afford something better. She does not seem to be working. Jo's reference to her 'immoral earnings' implies that she takes money from men she sleeps with.

How do Jo and Helen feel about being poor and what do they do about it?

Both of them want better lives and more money. Helen achieves this by marrying Peter. She offers Jo money and invites her to stay. She buys things for the baby.

When Jo leaves school, she goes to work. She tells Geof she is working in a shop and in a pub, but the flat is dirty and she is not taking care of herself. Although her jobs are not well-paid, Geof suggests that she is not poor but is not managing her money well. She can buy herself clothes and make-up but does not pay the rent.

Later, Geof finds her another job but she gives it up and lets Geof pay her rent. There is a parallel with Helen's situation. Jo is not **materialistic** as Helen; like her, she wants money but is not keen on hard work. Neither of them blames anyone else for their lack of money.

Key Quotations to Learn

Jo: You can afford something better than this old ruin.

Helen: When you start earning you can start moaning. (Act 1 Scene 1)

Geof: Got any money?

Jo: Only my wages and they don't last long. By the time I've bought all I need, stockings and make-up and things, I've got nothing left. (Act 2 Scene1)

Helen: She'd be better off working than living off you like a little bloodsucker. (Act 2 Scene 1)

Summary

- Helen and Jo do not have much money and live in poor-quality accommodation.
- Helen escapes poverty for a time by marrying Peter.
- Jo works in low-paid jobs and struggles to survive.
- Jo lets Geof pay her rent.

Sample Analysis

Helen and Jo's poverty is reflected in their environment. The flat is 'falling apart', implying Helen can afford nothing better. Peter's description of the area they live in shows that it is an undesirable address, where only poor people would live: 'Tenements, cemetery, slaughterhouse.' This **minor sentence**, consisting of three **nouns**, starts with a type of housing which was at the time associated with poverty and links it to two places associated with death. In Act 2, Jo associates poverty with dirt and neglect, using the adjectives 'dirty' and 'filthy' to describe the washing and the children she can see from the flat.

Questions

QUICK TEST
1. Who does Jo blame for her living conditions?
2. How does Helen escape from poverty?
3. What does Jo spend her money on when she is working?
4. Who pays the rent in Act 2?

EXAM PRACTICE
Using at least one of the 'Key Quotations to Learn', write a paragraph explaining how Delaney explores the theme of poverty in *A Taste of Honey*.

Creativity and Beauty

You must be able to: analyse how ideas about creativity and beauty are presented in the play.

How are ideas about beauty presented in the play?

At the beginning, after commenting on the ugliness of the flat and the area, Jo attempts to bring some beauty into the flat. She also produces some bulbs which she has stolen from the park and which she hopes will grow because 'It's nice to see a few flowers'. They are a symbol of hope, which is crushed when Jo neglects them and they do not grow.

Helen and Jo discuss the physical attractiveness of a 'handsome' boy who lives nearby and of Jo's boyfriend.

They also pay attention to their own looks. In Act 1 Scene 2, Helen spends a long time getting ready to go out with Peter, Jo calling her make-up 'the art work'. Later, Peter uses a similar metaphor to insult Helen, calling her a 'bloody unrestored oil painting'. In Act 1, when the Boy compliments her 'pretty neck', Jo mentions her 'schoolgirl complexion'. In Act 2 she tells Geof she needs make-up.

How is creativity presented in the play?

Jo's drawings show her creative side and her need to express herself through art. Helen's praise for them contrasts with Geof's more informed criticism. He is an art student and thinks she should 'go to a decent school', implying that creativity is not enough without training and work. He sees Jo's drawings as a reflection of her personality and lack of focus.

Jo also shows a creative side when she tells Geof stories about the Boy and her father, both of them fantasies. There is something childish about her creativity as there is about the books she owns.

Jo resents the job Geof gets her retouching photographs, thinking he did it to prove she was 'the artistic type'. Unlike her sketches, it is a practical use of any talent she might have.

Other examples of creativity used for practical purposes are the woman downstairs making a cot from wicker and Geof making clothes for the baby. Both of them use their talents to help others. Jo's drawings, in contrast, might be seen as inward looking and self-centred as they are mostly self-portraits.

Jo speaks of the baby as a creation of her and the Boy's love.

Key Quotations to Learn

Helen: Self-portraits? Oh! Well, I suppose you've got to draw pictures of yourself, nobody else would. (Act 1 Scene 1)

Geof: … They're exactly like you.

Jo: How do you mean?

Geof: Well, there's no design, rhythm or purpose. (Act 2 Scene 1)

Jo: … They say love creates. And I'm certainly creating at the moment. I'm going to have a baby. (Act 2 Scene 1)

Summary

- Jo tries to bring some beauty into her life.
- Jo's creativity reflects her character and attitude to life.
- Geof uses his creative talents for practical purposes.
- Jo speaks of having a baby as an act of creation.

Sample Analysis

Helen uses the flattering adjective 'talented' to describe Jo when she sees her pictures, which she describes as 'very artistic'. She uses Jo's creativity to try to connect with her but Jo rebuffs her, first using the **ironic** hyperbole of 'I'm geniused' and then snatching the picture, as if embarrassed by praise. When Helen suggests that Jo could make use of her talent by going to art school, Jo reacts by saying 'It's too late'. There is **dramatic irony** in this statement as the audience is aware that Jo is only 16 or 17, and her negative attitude supports Helen's assertion that she is 'wasting' herself.

Questions

QUICK TEST
1. What does Jo steal, hoping they will bring beauty into the flat?
2. How does Jo express her creativity?
3. What is the 'artistic' job that Geof finds for Jo?
4. How does the old woman downstairs express her creativity?

EXAM PRACTICE
Using at least one of the 'Key Quotations to Learn', write a paragraph explaining how creativity is explored in *A Taste of Honey*.

You must be able to: analyse how the themes of darkness and death are presented in the play.

What references to darkness are there?

At the end of Act 1 Scene 1, Jo will not go to the bathroom because she is afraid of the dark. She tells Helen she is only afraid of the darkness inside, not the darkness outside.

At the beginning of Act 1 Scene 2, Jo mentions that it is getting dark early.

At the start of Act 2, she does not want to put the light on in the flat.

She puts the bulbs in the dark to help them grow but she forgets about them and they die.

How is darkness presented?

At the end of Act 1 Scene 1, Jo declares a fear of 'the darkness inside houses'. It is not clear why she should only be afraid of darkness inside the house. Perhaps she is afraid of what goes on within families or even within her own mind. Helen sees her fear as childish and tells her she needs to grow out of it.

When she meets Jimmie, Jo says she likes the winter, implying that she welcomes darkness. The darkness reflects the fact that they keep their relationship secret.

In the second act, she doesn't want Geof to see the state of the flat. There is a sense she has been hiding away in the dark, suggesting her attitude to darkness 'inside' has changed.

Darkness is associated with the Boy, partly because of the colour of his skin but also because Jo associates him with Africa, sometimes referred to as the 'dark continent' at that time, reflecting the idea that to Europeans it was mysterious and perhaps frightening. For Jo, 'darkest Africa' does not have negative **connotations** but contributes to her ideas about the Boy's background, making him mysterious and exciting.

What references to death are there?

The flat is close to two places associated with death: the slaughterhouse and the cemetery.

Jo tells Helen about a dream she had that Helen had died.

Helen compares the bed to a coffin.

Jo talks about the baby being born dead and about killing it, and threatens to kill herself twice.

What attitudes to death are shown?

Jo's dream could suggest that she is worried about being left alone – Helen has abandoned her several times to go off with men and will again. Neither she nor Helen attempt to interpret the dream and Helen's reaction is light-hearted. Her comparison of the bed to a coffin is also humorous and she is matter of fact about the idea of dying.

When Jo is pregnant and worried about the future, her fear comes out in suggesting that the baby might be born dead and in the shocking scene where she attacks the doll and says that she will kill the baby. This reflects her pessimism and her **ambivalence** about the baby.

Key Quotations to Learn

Helen: Are you afraid of the dark?
Jo: You know I am.
Helen: You should try not to be. (Act 1 Scene 1)

Jo: ... He could sing and dance and he was as black as coal.
Geof: A black boy?
Jo: From darkest Africa! A Prince! (Act 2 Scene 1)

Jo: ... I'll bash its brains out. I'll kill it. I don't want his baby, Geof. I don't want to be a mother. I don't want to be a woman. (Act 2 Scene 2)

Summary

- Jo starts the play afraid of the dark.
- Later she says she likes the dark nights.
- Jo dreams about Helen's death and talks about the baby's death.

Sample Analysis

In Act 1 Scene 1, Helen jokes that the room will 'look all right in the dark', suggesting that the best way to deal with its **squalor** is to ignore it. She then makes the more general point that 'Everything is seen at its best in the dark – including me.' For her, darkness is associated with avoiding the truth both about her surroundings and herself. At the beginning of Act 2, Jo leaves the flat in darkness when Geof enters, ironically praising 'the romantic half-light'. Despite her earlier fear of darkness, she too wants to ignore the state of the flat and, by implication, her life.

Questions

QUICK TEST
1. What building associated with death is near the flat?
2. To what does Helen compare her bed?
3. How does Jo say she will kill the baby?

EXAM PRACTICE
Using at least one of the 'Key Quotations to Learn', write a paragraph explaining how Delaney presents the theme of darkness in *A Taste of Honey.*

Tastes of Honey

You must be able to: understand why the play is called *A Taste of Honey*.

Where does the play's title come from?

The play's title refers to a quotation from the Bible. Saul, the King of Israel, forbids his people to eat the day before a battle, saying anyone who does so will be cursed and will die. His son, Jonathan, does not hear and eats some honey.

When Saul finds out, Jonathan says: 'I did but taste a little honey with the end of the rod that was in my hand and, lo, I must die.' (First Book of Samuel, Chapter 14 Verse 43)

When he is taken by the enemy, Jonathan is prepared to die to fulfil his father's curse but he is rescued and so does not die.

What does the quotation mean?

The story can be read as meaning different things: that the people should not have been forbidden the pleasure of eating the honey; that pleasure leads to death; or that death is a price worth paying for a brief moment of pleasure. The fact that Jonathan is saved suggests that either God did not approve of Saul's curse or that Jonathan's heroic deeds outweighed his transgression.

In *A Taste of Honey,* nobody dies but there are several references to the inevitability of death. The title might suggest that pleasure must be paid for in some way or that life should be enjoyed because it is so short.

Who has a taste of honey in the play?

Jo's taste of honey is her brief love affair with the Boy, something religious people would see as sinful and so forbidden. Her pregnancy is the result of this and could be seen as her 'curse' but she does not regret the affair and remembering it makes her happy. It is a brief time of happiness in a hard life.

Helen also tastes happiness in her relationship with Peter. Although it ends badly, she enjoys herself and does not regret it. Her affair with Jo's father could be seen as a taste of honey for which she has been paying for the rest of her life.

Geof's stay with Jo can be seen as his taste of honey, a time when he is happier than ever before and feels useful and loved. Again, it does not last long.

Key Quotations to Learn

Jo: I may as well be naughty while I've got the chance. I'll probably never see you again. I know it. (Act 1 Scene 2)

Helen: Do you think I understand? For one night, actually it was the afternoon, I loved him. (Act 1 Scene 2)

Helen: You couldn't wait, could you? Now look at the mess you've landed yourself in. (Act 2 Scene 2)

Summary

- The title of the play is taken from the Bible.
- Jonathan tastes honey and, because of his father's curse, must die – but he is rescued.
- Jo's affair with the Boy is a moment of pleasure in a difficult life.
- Helen and Geof also taste happiness.

Sample Analysis

Helen reacts to finding Jo's Bible by referring to her 'credulity', implying that the Bible, like Jo's other books, is a childish fairy tale, and by quoting part of a common saying: 'Eat, drink and be merry.' This saying is usually finished with 'for tomorrow we die'. Although this is not a direct quotation from the Bible, like 'a taste of honey', it is a version of a biblical quotation and is used to mean that we might as well enjoy ourselves in the short time we have. Jo finishes the quotation differently with 'And live to regret it'. This could be seen as **foreshadowing** her own brief experience of happiness and its result. However, she makes it clear in Act 2 that she does not regret her moments of pleasure with the Boy.

Questions

QUICK TEST
1. What can be seen as Jo's 'taste of honey'?
2. Does Jo regret her experience of love?
3. What is Helen's 'taste of honey' during the play?
4. What was Helen's 'taste of honey' in the past?

EXAM PRACTICE
Using at least one of the 'Key Quotations to Learn', write a paragraph explaining how Delaney presents Jo's and Helen's feelings about Jo's 'taste of honey'.

Resilience

You must be able to: analyse how ideas about resilience are presented in the play.

What is resilience?

Resilience is the ability to recover from difficulties. Delaney wanted to show the resilience of working-class northern people.

How does Helen show resilience?

She does not moan about the flat but uses irony to describe the 'lovely view of the gas works', at the same time criticising and accepting it. The shared bathroom, the bed, the décor and even the idea of her own death are dealt with in a similar way.

She wants a better life but does not complain about poverty and, although sometimes angry with Jo, she is generally cheerful. She enjoys life.

Even when her brief marriage fails, she is not bitter. She dismisses Peter's new girlfriend humorously as a 'bit of crumpet' and reflects that it was 'good while it lasted'.

The only things that seem to shock her and make her angry are finding out about Jo's relationship and being told that the baby 'will be black'. However, she is able to accept the pregnancy, taking on the role of doting grandmother. She copes with the idea of the baby being black characteristically by making a joke.

She can be seen as fatalistic, accepting whatever life throws at her. She is a survivor.

How does Jo show resilience?

Like Helen, Jo reacts to adversity with ironic humour but she is less willing to accept things she does not like, such as the state of the flat or her mother's attitude to her.

She shares some of Helen's fatalism, shown when she tells Jimmie that she does not expect him to return, but she is emotional and changeable. The prospect of having a baby at times depresses or frightens her but at other times she is optimistic about the future.

Jo also uses hyperbole, exaggerating the difficulties she faces, causing Helen to describe her as a 'tragedy queen' and to unsympathetically urge her to stop feeling sorry for herself and get on with life. At the end, alone on the stage, she is doing just that. There has been no tragedy and life goes on.

Key Quotations to Learn

Helen: Listen to it! Still, we all have funny ideas at that age, don't we – makes no difference though, we all end up the same way sooner or later. (Act 1 Scene 1)

Helen: All right, you thought you knew it all before, didn't you? But you came a cropper. Now it's 'poor little Josephine, the tragedy queen, hasn't life been hard on her'. Well, you fell down, you get up … nobody else is going to carry you about. (Act 2 Scene 1)

Jo: … We don't ask for life, we have it thrust upon us. (Act 2 Scene 2)

Summary

- Resilience means the ability to cope with and recover from difficulties.
- Both Helen and Jo use ironic humour to help them cope.
- Helen has a fatalistic view of the world.
- Jo becomes more resilient as the play goes on.

Sample Analysis

In Act 2 Scene 1, Helen calls Jo a 'tragedy queen' and refers to her situation as a 'Victorian melodrama', the theatrical metaphors implying that Jo's emotions are exaggerated and she is enjoying feeling like a victim. Helen is unsympathetic: 'you fell down, you get up.' She uses an everyday metaphor to criticise her for not being resilient. Despite some more emotional incidents in Scene 2, such as throwing the doll to the ground, Jo downplays her situation at the end of the play by saying that 'there's no trouble' and that pregnancy is 'a perfectly normal, healthy function'. Given her previous behaviour, there is some irony in these assertions. Nevertheless, she appears more resilient than she was earlier.

Questions

QUICK TEST
1. What form of humour does Helen use to help her cope?
2. What frightens and depresses Jo?
3. Why does Helen call Jo a 'tragedy queen'?
4. Which character can be described as fatalistic?

EXAM PRACTICE
Using at least one of the 'Key Quotations to Learn', write a paragraph explaining how Helen's resilience is presented in A Taste of Honey.

You must be able to: analyse how women's and men's roles are presented in the play.

How are women's roles presented in the play?

The play's two main characters are women. Most plays written before *A Taste of Honey* were dominated by male characters.

Helen and Jo can be seen as being disadvantaged in society because of their sex. They work in low-paid jobs without prospects. They depend on men for financial support. It can be argued that lack of opportunities for women force them into this role but it can also be argued that Jo chooses to live like this: she leaves school early out of choice.

In some ways, they conform to traditional gender roles: they both want to get married, they both like clothes and make-up, and they both let men make decisions for them.

In other ways, they do not conform. At the beginning and end of the play, they are together without a man. Neither of them has support from the father of her child. Helen expects Jo to work to look after the baby and herself. In the second act, Jo says she does not want a man in her life. Helen has not been a conventional mother, and says mothers are not responsible for their children. Neither of them shows much interest in 'home making', though Helen's attitude changes towards the end of the play when she embraces a traditional 'grandmother' role.

Jo is determined to be independent and make her own decisions, saying that she knows what she wants. In this way, she is a strong female character but she does not say what it is she wants and the 'open' ending leaves the audience wondering what the future will hold for her.

How are men's roles presented in the play?

The men in the play are secondary characters. Peter and the Boy take on traditional male roles, both with careers and both apparently willing to marry and support their wives (though the Boy does not marry Jo). They might seem like opposites – the Boy gentle and charming; Peter loud and aggressive – but neither accepts responsibility. Jo refers to the Boy as a little boy in an indulgent way. Helen indulges Peter's drinking and womanising. Their lack of commitment and apparent immaturity make them seem weak.

Geof is more reliable and, in looking after Jo, takes on a traditional male role. Jo jokes about him being her husband and her baby's father. However, he also takes on the traditionally female roles of shopping, cleaning and sewing. Because of his sexuality, some might see this as stereotypical.

Key Quotations to Learn

Jo: ... Don't little boys carry some trash. (Act 1 Scene 2)

Geof: What sort of a woman is she?
Jo: She's all sorts of woman. (Act 2 Scene 1)

Geof: Yes, the one thing civilisation couldn't do anything about – women. (Act 2 Scene 2)

Summary

- *A Taste of Honey* was unusual in having two women as the main characters.
- Helen and Jo are reliant on each other, not men, at the start and the end of the play.
- In some ways they conform to traditional gender roles.
- The men in the play, except for Geof, are unreliable.

Sample Analysis

The Boy tells Jo that 'Women ... are born three thousand years old.' His meaning is unclear but his hyperbole suggests that he thinks women are more mature than men and might have inborn wisdom and instincts that men do not have. Just as he is something of a mystery to Jo because of his ethnicity, she is a mystery to him because of her sex. This idea that there is a fundamental difference between the sexes is reiterated by Geof in his exasperated final line: 'Yes, the one thing civilisation couldn't do anything about – women'. His use of the **abstract noun** 'civilisation' implies that women are more natural and less easily subdued than men.

Questions

QUICK TEST
1. Are the main characters male or female?
2. In what way do the jobs Jo does reflect traditional gender roles?
3. Which two male characters are unreliable?
4. Name three traditionally female tasks Geof performs.

EXAM PRACTICE
Using at least one of the 'Key Quotations to Learn', write a paragraph explaining how Delaney writes about men in *A Taste of Honey*.

Tips and Assessment Objectives

You must be able to: understand how to approach the exam question and meet the requirements of the mark scheme.

Quick Tips

- You will get a choice of two questions. Do the one that best matches your knowledge, the quotations you have learned and the things you have revised.

- Make sure you know what the question is asking you. Underline key words and pay particular attention to the bullet point prompts that come with the question.

- You should spend about 45 minutes on your response. Allow yourself five minutes to plan your answer so there is some structure to your essay, leaving 40 minutes to write the essay.

- All your paragraphs should contain a clear idea, a relevant reference to the play (ideally a quotation) and analysis of how Delaney conveys the idea. Whenever possible, you should link your comments to the play's context.

- It can sometimes help, after each paragraph, to quickly re-read the question to keep yourself focused on the exam task.

- Keep your writing concise. If you waste time 'waffling' you won't be able to include the full range of analysis and understanding that the mark scheme requires.

- It is a good idea to remember what the mark scheme is asking of you.

AO1: Understand and respond to the play (12 marks)

This is all about coming up with a range of points that match the question, supporting your ideas with references to the play and writing your essay in a mature, academic style.

Lower	Middle	Upper
The essay has some good ideas that are mostly relevant. Some quotations and references are used to support the ideas.	A clear essay that always focuses on the exam question. Quotations and references support ideas effectively. The response refers to different points in the play.	A convincing, well-structured essay that answers the question fully. Quotations and references are well-chosen and integrated into sentences. The response covers the whole play (not everything, but ideas from throughout the play rather than just focusing on one or two sections).

AO2: Analyse the effects of Delaney's language, form and structure (12 marks)

You need to comment on how specific words, language techniques, sentence structures, stage directions or the narrative structure allow Delaney to get her ideas across to the audience. This could simply be something about a character or a larger idea she is exploring through the play. To achieve this, you will need to have learned good quotations to analyse.

Lower	Middle	Upper
Identification of some different methods used by Delaney to convey meaning. Some subject terminology.	Explanation of Delaney's different methods. Clear understanding of the effects of these methods. Accurate use of subject terminology.	Analysis of the full range of Delaney's methods. Thorough exploration of the effects of these methods. Accurate range of subject terminology.

AO3: Understand the relationship between the play and its contexts (6 marks)

For this part of the mark scheme, you need to show your understanding of how Delaney's ideas relate to the time when she was writing and the genre she wrote in.

Lower	Middle	Upper
Some awareness of how ideas in the play link to its contexts.	References to relevant aspects of contexts show a clear understanding.	Exploration is linked to specific aspects of the play's contexts to show a detailed understanding.

AO4: Written accuracy (4 marks)

You need to use accurate vocabulary, expression, punctuation and spelling. Although it is only four marks, this could make the difference between a lower or a higher grade.

Lower	Middle	Upper
Reasonable level of accuracy. Errors do not get in the way of the essay making sense.	Good level of accuracy. Vocabulary and sentences help to keep ideas clear.	Consistent high level of accuracy. Vocabulary and sentences are used to make ideas clear and precise.

1. How far does Delaney present Jo as an independent young woman in *A Taste of Honey*? Write about:
   • what Jo does and says in the play
   • how far Delaney presents her as being independent.

2. It has been said that *A Taste of Honey* is a play about society's misfits. How far do you agree with this view of the play? Write about:
   • what characters say and do in the play
   • how far Delaney presents them as misfits.

3. How does Delaney use the character of Helen to express ideas about motherhood and responsibility in *A Taste of Honey*? Write about:
   • what Helen says and does in the play
   • how Delaney uses her to express ideas about motherhood.

4. 'The relationship between Jo and Helen is difficult and dysfunctional but it is the only relationship that Jo can rely on.' How far do you agree with this statement? Write about:
   • how Delaney presents the relationship between Jo and Helen
   • how far you agree with the statement.

5. 'Peter is the least sympathetic character in *A Taste of Honey*.' How far do you agree with this statement? Write about:
   • what Peter says and does in the play
   • how far you agree with the statement.

6. How far does Delaney present Jo as a victim in *A Taste of Honey*? Write about:
   • what happens to Jo in the play
   • how far Delaney presents Jo as a victim.

7. How does Delaney present ideas about marriage in *A Taste of Honey*? Write about:
   • what ideas about and attitudes to marriage are shown in the play
   • how Delaney presents these ideas by the way in which she writes.

8. How does Delaney present the relationship between Jo and the Boy in *A Taste of Honey*? Write about:
   • what Jo and the Boy's relationship is like
   • how Delaney presents their relationship by the ways in which she writes.

9. The ending of *A Taste of Honey* has been described as deliberately ambiguous and open. To what extent do you agree with this? Write about:
   • what is meant by the ending being ambiguous or open
   • to what extent you agree that it is open or ambiguous.

10. 'Geof is the least selfish character in *A Taste of Honey*.' How far do you agree with this statement? Write about:
    - what Geof says and does in the play
    - how far you agree that he is the least selfish character in the play.

11. Helen says 'Well, I've always said we should be used for manure when we're gone'. How does Delaney present ideas about death in *A Taste of Honey*? Write about:
    - what references to death there are in the play
    - how Delaney writes about death.

12. '*A Taste of Honey* is a play about how a brief moment of happiness changes Jo's life forever.' How far do you agree with this statement? Write about:
    - Jo's moment of happiness and how it changes her life
    - how far you agree with the statement.

13. 'Helen in *A Taste of Honey* is not a strong character but she is a survivor.' How far do you agree with this statement? Write about:
    - what Helen says and does in the play
    - how far you agree that Delaney presents her as not strong but a survivor.

14. 'In *A Taste of Honey*, Delaney presents men as weak and unreliable.' How far do you agree with this statement? Write about:
    - the male characters in *A Taste of Honey*, what they do and what they say
    - how far you agree with the statement.

15. How does Delaney explore ideas about poverty and deprivation in *A Taste of Honey*? Write about:
    - what ideas about poverty and deprivation are explored in the play
    - how Delaney presents these ideas by the ways in which she writes.

16. In *A Taste of Honey*, Geof tells Jo that she is just like Helen. Do you agree? Write about:
    - the similarities and differences between Jo and Helen
    - how Delaney presents their similarities and differences by the way she writes.

17. Is *A Taste of Honey* an optimistic or a pessimistic play? Write about:
    - ways in which *A Taste of Honey* can be described as being optimistic or pessimistic
    - how Delaney conveys optimism or pessimism by the way in which she writes.

18. 'In many ways, Jo in *A Taste of Honey* is a typical teenage girl of her time.' How far do you agree with this statement? Write about:
    - what Jo says and does in the play
    - to what extent you agree that she is a typical teenage girl of her time.

Planning a Character Question Response

You must be able to: understand what an exam question is asking you and prepare your response.

How might an exam question on character be phrased?

A typical character question will read like this:

How far does Delaney present Jo as an independent young woman in *A Taste of Honey*?

Write about:

- what Jo does and says in the play
- how far Delaney presents her as being independent.   [30 marks + 4 AO4 marks]

How do I work out what to do?

The focus of this question is clear: the character of Jo and whether she is independent.

'How far' is the key aspect of this question.

For AO1, you need to display a clear understanding of what Jo is like, how she acts and to what extent it is fair to describe her as independent.

For AO2, you need to analyse the different ways in which Delaney's use of language, structure and the dramatic form help to show the audience what Jo is like at different points in the play. Ideally, you should include quotations that you have learned but, if necessary, you can make a clear reference to a specific part of the play.

You also need to remember to link your comments to the play's context to achieve your AO3 marks and to write accurately to pick up your four AO4 marks for spelling, punctuation and grammar.

How can I plan my essay?

You have approximately 45 minutes to write your essay.

This isn't long but you should spend the first five minutes writing a quick plan. This will help you to focus your thoughts and produce a well-structured essay.

Try to come up with five or six ideas. Each of these ideas can then be written up as a paragraph.

You can plan in whatever way you find most useful. Some students like to just make a quick list of points and then re-number them into a logical order. Spider diagrams are particularly popular; look at the example on the next page.

Independent: Helen does not take responsibility for Jo so she looks after herself.
Not independent: Jo has not chosen this way of life.

Independent: In Act 1, she wants to leave school and earn a living.
Not independent: In Act 2, she cannot manage and relies on Geof.

Independent: She says she can bring up her baby alone.
Not independent: She is ambiguous about the baby's future – she lets both Geof and Helen plan for it.
Context: pregnancy and single mothers in the 1950s.

Is Jo independent?

Independent: Unconventional in her views. Makes up her own mind about people.

Independent: She says she does not want a man in her life.
Not independent: She is not alone through choice (the Boy does not return).

Independent: She says she is 'extraordinary' and knows what she wants but does not say what it is she wants – maybe she does not know.

Summary

- Make sure you know what the focus of the essay is.
- Remember to analyse how Delaney conveys her ideas.
- Try to relate your ideas to the play's social and historical context.

Questions

QUICK TEST
1. What key skills do you need to show in your answer?
2. What are the benefits of quickly planning your essay?
3. Why is it better to have learned quotations for the exam?

EXAM PRACTICE
Plan a response to the following question.
'Helen in *A Taste of Honey* is not a strong character but she is a survivor.' How far do you agree with this statement? Write about:
- what Helen says and does in the play
- how far you agree that Delaney presents her as not strong but a survivor.

How far does Delaney present Jo as an independent young woman in *A Taste of Honey*?

Write about:

- what Jo does and says in the play
- how far Delaney presents her as being independent. [30 marks + 4 AO4 marks]

From the start of the play, Jo comes across as an independent young woman who has to rely on herself and has her own opinions (1). Her first words are 'I don't like it.' This shows that she makes up her own mind about things (2). It is clear that she has to more or less look after herself. Her mother does not know much about what she does or care much about it, like the fact she has been stealing bulbs from the park. When she looks at Jo's drawings, it is the first time she has seen them or shown an interest. Jo has had to be independent (3).

Jo has made her mind up to leave school. She wants to earn a living and says to Helen that the first thing she will do is 'Get out of your sight as soon as I can get a bit of money in my pocket.' When she does leave school, she gets two jobs and lives on her own in the flat. In this way, she is independent. On the other hand, she is not managing very well. The flat is dirty. She is neglecting her health and not planning for the baby. She needs Geof to help her manage (4).

She also makes her own decisions about the baby. She has decided not to 'get rid' of it by having an abortion. It was unusual for an unmarried girl or woman in the 1950s to bring up a child alone so her decision to keep it is brave as well as independent. However, she does not definitely say she will not have the baby adopted, which was the most common option then, but when she says she might 'dump it on a doorstep' she is joking. Even not having plans can be a sign of independence as it shows she will decide what she wants to do herself (5).

When Helen returns to see her, she offers Jo money and a place to live. She shows she is proud and independent by refusing both, telling her 'you know what you can do with it'. Helen says that she is a 'bloodsucker', using a metaphor (6) to say she is living off Geof but Jo says that they share everything and are 'communists'. As we already know that she has given up work and has no maternity benefit, we might not believe this (7).

She shows that she thinks and acts independently in her relationship with the Boy. She keeps it from Helen. She shows she can think for herself by not minding that he is black at a time when people were racist and relationships between black and white people very unusual. Her attitude to Geof shows the same thing. They describe themselves as 'degenerates', meaning that society might think they were immoral people, but they are independent of society (8).

Even when the Boy is with her, she says she does not expect him to come back but she says she will be there. It is as if she expects to be alone. She later says she does not want to get married and does not want any man in her life. At the end of the play, she says she feels 'really important' and that she could 'take care of the whole world'. Earlier, she said she knew exactly what she wanted from life, showing she is confident and looks to the future. This sounds independent but it is vague (9).

At the very end of the play, she is alone on the stage, an image which gives a picture of an independent young woman coping with childbirth on her own but she has not chosen to be alone (10).

1. The essay starts with a clear focus on the question with a simple reference to structure. AO1/AO2

2. Reference effectively supports a straightforward idea. AO1

3. Clearly expands on ideas about the play with references to the text. AO1/AO2

4. Maintains focus on the question, particularly on 'how far'. AO1/AO2

5. Considers historical context, showing clear if unsophisticated understanding, and links to the text. AO1/AO3

6. Accurate terminology used to explain writer's methods. AO3

7. Still focuses on the question and explores another part of the play. Effective support from quotations. AO1

8. More references to context clearly linked to ideas about the play. AO1/AO3

9. Continues to focus on the question and makes valid points but lacks some coherence and could be more effectively supported with references to the text. Awareness of structure shown. AO1/AO2/AO4

10. Shows clear understanding of the writer's methods using appropriate terminology. The candidate has maintained focus on the question until the end, making a good attempt at answering 'how far' by considering whether Jo's actions show she is independent. AO1/AO2/AO3

Questions

EXAM PRACTICE

Choose a paragraph of this essay. Read it through a few times then try to rewrite and improve it. You might:

- improve the sophistication of the language or the clarity of expression
- replace a reference with a quotation or use a better quotation
- provide more detailed, or a wider range of, analysis
- use more subject terminology
- link some context to the analysis more effectively.

A proportion of the best top-band answers will be awarded Grade 8 or Grade 9. To achieve this you should aim for a sophisticated, fluent and nuanced response that displays flair and originality.

How far does Delaney present Jo as an independent young woman in *A Taste of Honey*?

Write about:

- what Jo does and says in the play
- how far Delaney presents her as being independent.   [30 marks + 4 AO4 marks]

Jo's first words in the play are 'And I don't like it', responding to Helen's opening line with a blunt negative statement (1). The following dialogue establishes that her relationship with Helen is not that of a dependent, obedient child. She questions why she should 'run around after' her mother and treats her as an equal, calling her by her first name. Her exclamation 'What I wouldn't give for a room of my own!' shows a desire for both privacy and independence. In some ways, however, Jo already lives quite an independent life. Helen does not know or care much about what she does. When she looks at Jo's drawings, it is the first time she has seen them and Jo rebuffs her interest. The fact that most of these drawings are self-portraits might indicate self-reliance bordering on selfishness (2).

Jo further asserts her desire for independence by wanting to leave school and Helen is not willing or able to stop her, using the **colloquial** *phrase 'set on' to express Jo's determination (3). Jo says the first thing she will do after leaving school is 'Get out of your sight as soon as I can get a bit of money in my pocket.' However, her choice is really a negative one – the important things are not being at school and not living with Helen. There is no sense of ambition or even planning for the future (4).*

When she does leave school, she gets two jobs and lives on her own in the flat. She is now independent but it is not through choice. After Helen leaves with Peter, Jo is seen 'crying on the bed': an image of an abandoned child rather than an independent young woman. She is keen for the Boy to stay with her over Christmas, recalling the previous times when she has been left alone by Helen. He too abandons her, however, and again she is forced to be independent.

At the beginning of Act Two she is alone and financially independent but she is not managing very well. When Geof tells her 'You want taking in hand', using a colloquial phrase that implicitly criticises her ability to cope, she resists at first. However, she suggests he moves in – though she presents the offer as doing him a favour – and allows herself to be taken 'in hand', becoming increasingly dependent on him. There is a disconnection between what she says and what she does. She wants to be independent but is not really able to live independently (5).

In her attitude to her pregnancy, Jo shows some independence of mind in deciding not to 'get rid' of the baby by having an abortion. It was unusual for an unmarried girl or woman in the 1950s to bring up a child alone so her keeping it can be seen as brave as well as independent. On the other hand, she has made no alternative plans and she even refers jokingly to leaving the baby 'on a doorstep' (6). Her assertion that there is no point in planning because the baby might be born 'dead or daft' – typically covering her fear with humour – leaves the audience in the dark about her intentions. This does not give the impression of an independent young woman.

When Helen offers Jo money and a place to live, she proudly refuses help, telling her 'you know what you can do with it', a crude innuendo that expresses her resentment of Helen's interference. Helen does not believe she is financially independent, using the metaphor 'bloodsucker' to accuse her of living off Geof (7). Jo's response that they share everything and are 'communists', while spirited, might not convince the audience as we already know she has no income. Furthermore, she does accept Helen's help at the end of the play, just as she accepted Geof's help despite telling him she could manage without him (8).

Although the events of the play tend to show that Jo is not independent in practical ways, she does display the ability to think for herself and defy convention. She tells Geof that she does not want a husband or any man in her life, which is unusual for the time when the play was written. Equally unconventional is her tolerant view of both the Boy's race and Geof's sexuality. Jo says that she and Geof are 'degenerates', meaning that society might think they were immoral but she is happy to live outside conventional society (9).

The play's final image of a smiling Jo alone on the stage, about to give birth, can be seen as a picture of an independent young woman coping with whatever life brings but, just as at the end of Act One, she has not chosen to be alone. The open ending may leave the audience wondering whether Jo can ever truly be independent (10).

1. The essay starts with a clear focus on the question, supported by a quotation and a comment on the writer's use of language. AO1/AO2
2. Develops the point effectively, referring closely to the text and focusing on 'how far'. AO1
3. Comment on the writer's methods (language). AO2
4. Maintains focus on the question, with thoughtful consideration of 'how far'. AO1
5. Convincing consideration of the question, using references to the text effectively and focusing on different parts of the play. AO2
6. Reference to a specific aspect of historical context linked to the text, showing clear understanding. AO3
7. Accurate terminology used to analyse the writer's methods. AO3
8. Still focuses on the question, exploring another part of the play. Effective support from quotations. AO1
9. More references to context clearly and effectively linked to ideas about the play. AO1/AO3
10. Effective analysis of the writer's stagecraft using appropriate terminology. The candidate has maintained focus on the question until the end, effectively exploring the question of 'how far' by considering the evidence thoughtfully. The writing has been clear and accurate throughout. AO1/AO2/AO4

Questions

EXAM PRACTICE

Spend 45 minutes writing an answer to the following exam question. Use the plan you prepared earlier.

'Helen in A Taste of Honey is not a strong character but she is a survivor.' How far do you agree with this statement? Write about:

*   what Helen says and does in the play
*   how far you agree that Delaney presents her as not strong but a survivor.

Planning a Theme Question Response

You must be able to: understand what an exam question is asking you and prepare your response.

How might an exam question on theme be phrased?

A typical theme question will read like this:

Helen says 'Well, I've always said we should be used for manure when we're gone.' How does Delaney present ideas about death in *A Taste of Honey*?

Write about:

- what references to death there are in the play
- how Delaney writes about death.   [30 marks + 4 AO4 marks]

How do I work out what to do?

The focus of this question is clear: ideas about death, and how they are presented.

'What' and 'how' are important elements of this question.

For AO1, 'what' shows that you need to display a clear understanding of the references to death and attitudes shown towards death in the play.

For AO2, 'how' shows that you need to analyse the ways in which Delaney's use of language, structure and the dramatic form present this theme to the audience at different points in the play. Ideally, you should include quotations that you have learned but, if necessary, you can make a clear reference to a specific part of the play.

You also need to remember to link your comments to the play's context to achieve your AO3 marks and to write accurately to pick up your four AO4 marks for spelling, punctuation and grammar.

How can I plan my essay?

You have approximately 45 minutes to write your essay.

This isn't long but you should spend the first five minutes writing a quick plan. This will help you to focus your thoughts and produce a well-structured essay.

Try to come up with five or six ideas. Each of these ideas can then be written up as a paragraph.

You can plan in whatever way you find most useful. Some students like to just make a quick list of points and then re-number them into a logical order. Spider diagrams are particularly popular; look at the example on the next page.

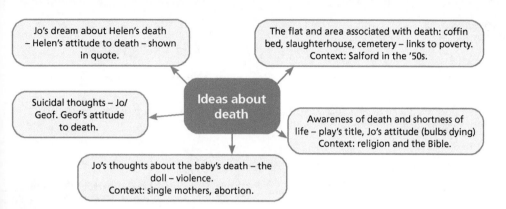

Jo's dream about Helen's death – Helen's attitude to death – shown in quote.

The flat and area associated with death: coffin bed, slaughterhouse, cemetery – links to poverty. Context: Salford in the '50s.

Ideas about death

Suicidal thoughts – Jo/Geof. Geof's attitude to death.

Awareness of death and shortness of life – play's title, Jo's attitude (bulbs dying) Context: religion and the Bible.

Jo's thoughts about the baby's death – the doll – violence. Context: single mothers, abortion.

Summary

- Make sure you know what the focus of the essay is.
- Remember to analyse how Delaney conveys her ideas.
- Try to relate your ideas to the play's social and historical context.

Questions

QUICK TEST
1. What key skills do you need to show in your answer?
2. What are the benefits of quickly planning your essay?
3. Why is it better to have learned quotations for the exam?

EXAM PRACTICE
Plan a response to the following question.
Is *A Taste of Honey* an optimistic or a pessimistic play? Write about:

- ways in which *A Taste of Honey* can be described as being optimistic or pessimistic
- how Delaney conveys optimism or pessimism by the way in which she writes.

Grade 5 Annotated Response

Helen says 'Well, I've always said we should be used for manure when we're gone.' How does Delaney present ideas about death in *A Taste of Honey*?

Write about:

- what references to death there are in the play
- how Delaney writes about death.   [30 marks + 4 AO4 marks]

The quote in the question comes after Jo tells Helen about her dream. In the dream, Jo is standing in a garden when she sees a policeman digging. They find Helen's body under a rose bush. This shows that Jo is worried about Helen dying or leaving her. She might be worried about dying herself, which would fit in with her fear of the dark. Helen is not bothered by the dream and makes a joke out of it. Saying that people's bodies should be 'used for manure' might seem disrespectful but it shows that Helen is not religious or sentimental. This fits in with what she said earlier about Jo's bulbs and how we all end up in a cool dark place but there's no point in worrying about it (1).

There are a few other references to death in the first scene after Jo and Helen move into the flat. Jo wonders if they'll live until the next day because of the roof leaking. The conditions they live in are very bad, as for lots of people at the time, and could affect their health (2). The flat is near the slaughterhouse where animals are killed and also near the cemetery, so death is all around them. Helen describes the bed as being 'like a coffin', a comparison which reminds us of death as they go to bed (3).

Nobody actually dies in 'A Taste of Honey' but on two separate occasions Jo threatens to take her own life. First she tells Geof that she feels like throwing herself in the river. It is hard to know how serious she is. Earlier, Geof told her she was depressed but now he jokes about it and her mood changes. Later she tells Helen she wants to jump out of the window but this is in the middle of a row and perhaps she is being the 'tragedy queen' that Helen accuses her of being. Geof might also have thought about suicide as he tells Jo that before he met her he did not care whether he lived or died (4).

Jo is worried that her baby will be born 'dead or daft' and is happy when she feels it kick, showing it is alive, but then, when Geof gives her the doll, she suddenly becomes violent. She throws down the doll and says she will kill the baby when it is born by bashing its brains out. This is a shocking scene for the audience, (5) especially as Jo was anxious about the baby before and seemed to want it. She told Geof that to 'get rid' of it by abortion would be 'terrible'. This might show that she is confused or depressed or just very nervous about her situation. For a young single woman to have a baby was frowned on then and you can understand her saying she did not want to be a mother (6). However, she seems to have a fascination with death and especially the baby's death (7).

*Religious beliefs about death are referred to several times, although nobody in the play is religious, reflecting how people were becoming less religious when the play was written (8). Helen is cynical about religion and makes fun of the idea of Heaven, saying she does not want to go there as it will be full of reformed sinners and their 'little tin god'. Geof thinks we come, we go and that's it. Jo is also cynical, although she reads the Bible and talks about people praying just in case God turns out to exist when they 'snuff it'. The **slang** phrase for death makes it seem as if she does not care about death but she may be using humour to avoid thinking about it seriously, as she and Helen do about many things (9). The characters do not dwell on death but are aware that life is short, reflecting the title, which is based on a biblical quote. They can enjoy a taste of honey for a short time but in the end we all die (10).*

1. The opening paragraph focuses on the question, particularly Helen's attitude, using a quotation and reference to support the points made. AO1

2. Some contextual understanding linked to the text. AO3

3. Relevant quotation; some understanding of the writer's methods and their effects. AO1/AO2

4. This paragraph could be more focused on the question. It does not really explore ideas about death. It does refer to different parts of the play and points are supported by reference to the text. AO2/AO4

5. Clear understanding of the effect of Delaney's methods. AO2

6. Quotation linked to context but its relevance to the question is not very clear. AO3

7. Attempt to focus on the question. This paragraph has covered another part of the play. AO1

8. Reference to a relevant aspect of context. AO3

9. Quotation used to support point made and correct use of terminology to analyse writer's methods. Clear focus on the question. Explanation of Delaney's methods (language). AO1/ AO2

10. The candidate has written about many different parts of the play and mostly stayed focused on the question but the answer is lacking in analysis and spends too much time 'story telling'. Written expression is clear but could be more precise and coherent. AO1/AO3/AO4

> ## Questions
>
> Choose a paragraph of this essay. Read it through a few times then try to rewrite and improve it. You might:
> - improve the sophistication of the language or the clarity of expression
> - replace a reference with a quotation or use a better quotation
> - provide more detailed, or a wider range of, analysis
> - use more subject terminology
> - link some context to the analysis more effectively.

Grade 7+ Annotated Response

A proportion of the best top-band answers will be awarded Grade 8 or Grade 9. To achieve this you should aim for a sophisticated, fluent and nuanced response that displays flair and originality.

Helen says 'Well, I've always said we should be used for manure when we're gone.' How does Delaney present ideas about death in *A Taste of Honey*?

Write about:

- what references to death there are in the play
- how Delaney writes about death.

[30 marks + 4 AO4 marks]

*Helen's assertion that people should be 'used as manure' after death shows an unsentimental attitude to death. The word 'manure' picks up on the **imagery** of Jo's dream, in which Helen's body is found under a rose bush. The dream reflects a pessimistic side of Jo's character that contrasts with Helen's determination to enjoy life. Jo's dream might be expressing anxiety about the prospect of Helen abandoning her, as she has in the past, or could be designed merely to upset Helen. If the latter is true, Jo fails as Helen responds with her usual down-to-earth humour (1).*

Later, Jo wonders if they'll live until the next day because of the roof leaking. While this is hyperbole, it does bring into focus the poor housing conditions that Jo and Helen suffer, like many others at the time, and the serious consequences these conditions could have. The poverty of their environment is emphasised by references to the slaughterhouse and cemetery, two concrete reminders of the inevitability and the closeness of death (2). Helen jokes that, like Jo's bulbs, we will all end up in a 'cool, dark place', an image that recalls Jo's dream about the garden; she also compares the bed that they share to a coffin. These darkly comic images reflect both Helen's awareness of the inevitability of death and her acceptance of that fact (3).

Jo's attitude to death is more complex than Helen's. In the second act, she references suicidal thoughts on two separate occasions. First she tells Geof that she feels like throwing herself in the river. He makes a joke out of it, saying that the river is 'full of rubbish' and, when she says she too is rubbish, accuses her of self-pity. Later, Jo tells Helen she wants to jump out of the window. Again, she is not taken seriously. Helen, like Geof, accuses Jo of self-pity ('poor little Josephine') and considers her language and actions melodramatic, calling her a 'tragedy queen'. While Helen's reaction is characteristic of her relationship with Jo, Geof's is surprising. Earlier he said that he thought Jo was depressed and that before he met her he did not care whether he lived or died, so the audience might expect him to be more sympathetic. The fact that he is not suggests that he too does not take her threats seriously (4).

*Geof takes her threats to the baby more seriously: the scene where Jo attacks the baby doll has great visual impact, and is shocking to the audience (5). Previously, Jo has appeared to want the baby despite the social stigma of being an unmarried mother. She rejects the idea of abortion as 'terrible'. She is happy when she feels it kick. However, thoughts of death are associated with the baby when she voices her fear that it will be born 'dead or daft'. Now she says she will 'bash its brains out', the **alliterative** phrase sounding brutal as the words are almost spat out. Violent death is again seen as a way out of life's problems and the threat of it used as a way of expressing Jo's frustration and fear about the future (6).*

Neither Geof nor Helen tell Jo that suicide and murder are morally wrong. They do not adhere to conventional religious beliefs. Their attitudes reflect a time when more and more people were questioning traditional religion (7). Helen ridicules the idea of life after death, with the **plosives** *of her humorous alliterative list of 'pimps, prostitutes and politicians' expressing her contempt for both the 'reformed sinners' and their 'little tin god' who she thinks she might find in a Christian Heaven. Geof thinks 'you come, you go, it's simple' and does not dwell on thoughts of death. Jo is also cynical, although she reads the Bible, and talks of people using religion as an 'insurance policy' just in case God turns out to exist when they 'snuff it'. This colloquialism suggests that she does not care about death although she may be using humour to avoid confronting a serious issue, something she and Helen often do (8).*

Nobody dies in 'A Taste of Honey' and the characters do not dwell on death. However, they often use imagery and references that reflect an awareness of the brevity of life and the inevitability of death. Early in the play, Helen gives her philosophy as 'Eat, drink and be merry', a saying that is usually finished with 'for tomorrow we die', and the title of the play, taken from the Bible, refers to the idea that after a brief taste of honey (or pleasure) we must die. Delaney's characters are conscious of how fragile life is and how little time they have on earth (9) (10).

1. The opening paragraph focuses on the question. Quotation and reference are used effectively to support the points made. The approach is analytical and acknowledges alternative interpretations. AO1/AO2
2. Contextual understanding effectively linked to the text. AO3
3. Relevant quotations analysed, showing appreciation of the writer's methods and their effects. AO1/AO2
4. Considers another aspect of the theme, still focused on the question, and explores other parts of the text. The writer's methods are explored using correct terminology and quotations are used effectively. AO1/ AO2
5. Appreciation of Delaney's stagecraft and its effect. AO2
6. Detailed analysis of Delaney's use of language, based on well-chosen and integrated quotations. Accurate use of terminology. AO1/AO2
7. Analysis of themes linked to specific aspects of context. AO1/AO3
8. Quotations used effectively to support points made and correct use of terminology to analyse writer's methods. Clear focus on the question. Detailed analysis. AO1/ AO2
9. Thoughtful consideration of the question and analysis of the theme, showing quite a sophisticated understanding of the play. AO1
10. The candidate has written about the whole play and stayed focused on the question, analysing ideas and methods effectively and convincingly. Written expression is precise and coherent. AO1/AO3/AO4

Questions

EXAM PRACTICE

Spend 45 minutes writing an answer to the following exam question. Use the plan you have already prepared.

Is *A Taste of Honey* an optimistic or a pessimistic play? Write about:

- ways in which *A Taste of Honey* can be described as being optimistic or pessimistic
- how Delaney conveys optimism or pessimism by the way in which she writes.

Glossary

Abstract noun – a noun that names an idea, concept or emotion.

Adjective – a limiting or describing word.

Admonishment – a telling off.

Alliteration (*adj.* alliterative) – a series of words beginning with the same sound.

Ambiguous (*noun* ambiguity) – having more than one meaning or interpretation.

Ambivalence (*adj.* ambivalent) – having mixed feelings or contradictory ideas.

Angry Young Men (the) – a name given to some writers in the 1950s who were considered rebellious and controversial.

Antagonist – the person in a story who opposes the protagonist.

Antonym – a word that means the opposite of another word.

Brechtian – theatre style associated with the German playwright Bertolt Brecht (1898–1956).

Chronological order – ordered according to time.

Circular structure – when the end of a story recalls the beginning.

Colloquial (*adj.*) – (of speech) informal or chatty.

Confidant – a person someone confides in.

Conjunction – a joining word, e.g. and, or, but.

Connotation – an implied meaning or something suggested by association.

Contractions – (in childbirth) shortening of the muscles that occurs before and during childbirth.

Convention (*adj.* conventional) – the way in which something is usually done.

Derogatory – insulting.

Dialect – words or phrases particular to a region.

Dialogue – speech between two or more people; conversation.

Dramatic irony – a situation where the audience knows something that a character or characters do not know.

Elitism (*adj.* elitist) – a belief in the superiority of a small section of society, usually wealthier, more powerful and better educated than most.

Euphemism (*adj.* euphemistic) – the use of mild or vague expressions instead of harsh or blunt ones.

Exposition – the opening part of a novel or play where the setting and characters are introduced.

Fantasy – a story or idea that is made up.

Fatalism (*adj.* fatalistic) – a belief that the future is predetermined and cannot be changed.

Foreshadow – to anticipate or indicate a future event.

Fourth wall – in theatre, the idea that between the action and the audience there is an invisible wall.

House style – a style of writing or production which is typical of a particular theatre.

Hyperbole (*adj.* hyperbolic) – exaggeration.

Image – a picture.

Imagery – the use of words to create 'pictures'.

Imperative – an order or command.

Imply – to suggest something that is not expressly stated.

Improvisation – rehearsing or performing a play without a script or any preparation.

Industrial Revolution – the period of history (eighteenth to nineteenth century) when industry expanded rapidly.

Innuendo – a remark that hints at something (often sexual).

Interrogate – to question someone (often aggressively).

Irony (*adj.* ironic) – where words are used to imply an opposite meaning.

Kitchen sink drama – a naturalistic style of drama featuring ordinary people in everyday situations.

Materialistic (*noun* materialism) – being focused on money and/or possessions.

Melodrama (*adj.* melodramatic) – a style of theatre, popular in the Victorian era, featuring extreme situations and exaggerated acting.

Metaphor (*adj.* metaphorical) – an image created by writing about something as if it were another thing.

Minor sentence – a 'sentence' that does not include a verb, also called a fragment.

Music hall – a form of entertainment popular in the nineteenth and early twentieth centuries featuring a variety of acts such as singers, dancers, comedians, magicians and acrobats.

National Service – a system that operated in the UK from 1949 to 1963 under which 18-year-old men were required to serve for two years in the armed forces.

Naturalism (*adj.* naturalistic) – a style of theatre that seeks to reproduce real life as closely as possible.

Norm (*adj.* normal) – something that is usual or standard.

Noun – a naming word for a person, place, animal or object.

Parallel phrasing – repetition of similar sentence structures or word order.

Pejorative – expressing contempt or disapproval.

Philanderer – a man who has a lot of sexual affairs with different women.

Phrase – any group of words.

Platonic – adjective used to describe a relationship that does not involve sex.

Plosive – a sound made by a sudden release of air (such as 'p' or 't').

Popular theatre – a vague term for theatre aimed at or appealing to a wide range of people, especially working-class people.

Prejudice – a (usually negative) opinion of someone or something based on an already-formed idea rather than fact or observation.

Props (short for 'properties') – objects used on stage.

Prosaic – everyday, ordinary.

Protagonist – the main character.

Public image – the impression the public has of a well-known person.

Rhetorical question – a question that does not require an answer.

Secondary modern school – a school for pupils who failed to get a place in a grammar school after taking the 'eleven plus' exam.

Second person – 'you' (in both the singular and the plural).

Sentimental – showing or affected by emotion.

Sibilance – the hissing sound created by the letter 's', often used alliteratively.

Simile – a type of imagery that compares one thing to another using 'like' or 'as'.

Slang – informal speech.

Social stigma – disapproval of a person or group of people by society at large.

Sparring partners – two people who have serious but friendly arguments; an expression taken from boxing where two boxers who practise together are 'sparring partners'.

Squalor – the state of being very dirty and neglected.

Stereotype (*adj.* stereotypical) – a widely held but fixed and oversimplified idea, usually about a group of people.

Symbol – an object used to represent an idea.

Tenements – buildings containing flats, usually rented.

Traditional – long established.

Turning point – a point in a story when things change significantly.

Answers

Pages 4–5
Quick Test
1. She does not like it.
2. She puts her scarf over the naked light bulb.
3. Leave school
4. Helen's boyfriend, a car salesman

Exam Practice
Answers might refer to the way they enter with baggage; how they immediately disagree about the flat; how Jo resents being told what to do by Helen; the fact that they are mother and daughter; Jo calling Helen by her first name; the sense that they often move; the remarks that Helen addresses to the audience about Jo.

Analysis might include the visual impact of the set and of the characters' entrance; Jo's immediate response with half a sentence in reply to Helen's observation; Helen's question to Jo **implying** she is not very concerned about her leaving school; Jo's two **rhetorical questions** which draw attention to Helen's selfishness.

Pages 6–7
Quick Test
1. She might not want to be seen with him because he is black.
2. Jealousy
3. Jo and the Boy
4. She is angry, saying that Jo is stupid and is ruining her life.

Exam Practice
Answers might refer to how Peter attempts to win her over with chocolates; Jo's resentment of Peter; how she flirts with him but also attacks him physically; how he is disturbed by this and tries to control her; how Helen puts Jo's reaction down to jealousy.

Analysis might include Helen's use of the **metaphor** 'cat' with 'jealous' to imply Jo's viciousness; how this shows she takes Peter's side against Jo and values her relationship with him more than her relationship with her daughter, causing resentment from Jo; Helen's use of **sibilance** after Jo's refusal to kiss her ('I don't suppose you're sorry to see') suggesting a wheedling, softer tone and Jo's expression of indifference in response.

Pages 8–9
Quick Test
1. Geof
2. Art
3. Geof has asked her because he is worried about Jo.
4. A 'bloody slut'

Exam Practice
Answers might refer to their almost childish friendship; her motivations for asking him to stay; her curiosity about his lifestyle; his taking offence at what she says and her apology; the way he 'takes her in hand' and looks after her; his concern for her welfare; his attempt to kiss her; his devotion to her; his admission that he didn't care if she lived or died before meeting her; the way he fetches Helen out of concern for Jo.

Analysis might include Jo's use of the term 'people like you', implying that she is more interested in Geof's sexuality than in him as a person; how the term 'like a big sister' stresses their

closeness and the platonic nature of their relationship while stereotyping him; Geof's simple heartfelt appeal to Helen as Jo's mother, not anticipating her unsympathetic response.

Pages 10–11
Quick Test
1. He thinks that it is not true.
2. She becomes angry and upset, throwing the doll to the ground.
3. Peter is seeing another woman.
4. She is shocked but makes a joke out of it.

Exam Practice
Answers might refer to Geof's departure and Helen's exit; Jo being alone on the stage at the end; the stage direction indicating that Jo remembers Geof when she recites the nursery rhyme; the nursery rhyme itself; Jo's contractions; Helen's response and reaction to hearing the baby may be black.

Analysis might include the use of **circular structure** indicated by 'we're back where we started'; the openness of the ending; Geof's selflessness in leaving and his warning to Helen; Helen's lack of understanding of Jo expressed in the repeated negative 'I don't'; the breaking of the **'fourth wall'** to make the audience consider what they themselves might do in similar circumstances.

Pages 12–13
Quick Test
1. Jo and Helen
2. Helen leaving with Peter and the Boy moving in.
3. About ten months
4. Jo

Exam Practice
Similarities might include that Jo and Helen are in the same flat and living together; that they still fight; that Helen has once again left Peter. Differences might include Jo's pregnancy and the imminent birth of her baby; Helen having money to spend and appearing to want to care for Jo.

Analysis might include the repetition of 'loaded with baggage' in the stage directions, which illustrates the circular structure; 'as in Act One, Scene One' showing that the audience is meant to register the similarity; the fact that Helen now enters alone as Jo is already in the flat, now living with Geof.

Pages 14–15
Quick Test
1. Salford, Lancashire
2. Usherette
3. Samuel Beckett and Arthur Miller
4. They were not intended to be typical or representative of the area.

Exam Practice
Answers might include a comparison between Jo leaving school and Delaney's own experience; Jo's lack of formal education partly due to moving between schools; Jo's lack of interest in education; Jo's choice to work rather than stay at school (possible because of the availability of low-paid jobs); Jo's resistance to Helen's suggestion that she should go to art school; the contrast with Geof, who is studying art and has a more disciplined and organised approach than Jo.

Analysis might include Helen's use of interrogatives to get information from Jo; Jo's one-syllable reply to the first question, showing that her mind is made up and her second answer, which humorously implies that Helen cannot bear the sight of her and focuses on her motivation – 'money in my pocket', showing that she sees that as more important than school.

Pages 16–17
Quick Test
1. Bertolt Brecht
2. Music hall
3. *Look Back in Anger*
4. No

Exam Practice

Answers might refer to the Theatre Workshop's concept of popular theatre; music hall; the use of song to make the show entertaining; the presence of an orchestra or band; the actor's interaction with the orchestra.

Analysis might include Helen's use of the theatrical metaphor 'bring the house down' and the musical term (associated with jazz) 'vamp it up', indicating Helen is giving a performance for the audience; the stage direction 'To orchestra' that breaks the 'fourth wall'; the possibility that modern productions might not include a band and might ignore some of the more Brechtian elements of the script.

Pages 18–19
Quick Test
1. Yes
2. The flat and the street outside
3. By addressing the audience
4. No

Exam Practice

Answers might refer to the way music between the scenes indicates changes of time; how music and dancing entertain the audience; how directly addressing the audience gets people thinking about the issues.

Analysis might include the stage direction '*sings to the audience*' making it clear that the 'fourth wall' should be broken and the audience involved; directions for the actors to sing and dance lightening the mood and making the performance more fun; the impression Jo's smile might give the audience at the end; ways in which an actor might convey the idea that she is '*thinking of GEOF*'.

Pages 20–21
Quick Test
1. Cotton/textiles
2. Poor housing
3. The Manchester Ship Canal
4. Three from: the gasworks, the canal, the docks, tenements, the cemetery and the slaughterhouse.

Exam Practice

Answers might refer to the disrepair of the flat; its location near the gasworks; the problem of poor housing in the 1950s; Salford's industrial past shown in its landscape.

Analysis might include Helen's bald statement of fact about their conditions being balanced by humour in the second half of the sentence, introduced by the **conjunction** 'but'; using irony to describe the ugliness of their environment ('lovely view' and 'contemporary') and **euphemism** ('the community') to describe sharing with other lodgers.

Pages 22–23
Quick Test
1. Marriage or adoption
2. No

3. They all want to get married.
4. Not everyone at the time shared the same morality.

Exam Practice

Answers might refer to the fact that all five characters consider marriage and seem to aspire to it; Peter and Helen getting married; marriage being considered the norm in society at the time and the idea that it gave respectability to a relationship; both Peter and the Boy buying rings and proposing in a traditional way; Geof proposing marriage and seeking to conform despite his sexuality; ideas about men being responsible for their wives; Helen and Jo both having children outside marriage; Jo unconventionally deciding she does not want to marry; the brevity of Helen's marriage; Peter's unfaithfulness.

Pages 24–25
Quick Test
1. 1965
2. *Othello*
3. She is curious.
4. Peter and Helen

Exam Practice

Answers might refer to her being less concerned about it than he is; her curiosity about where he comes from; her (incorrect) assertion that Helen will not be prejudiced, showing naivety about the existence of racism; her use of stereotypical ideas about jungles and drums, which could be found offensive but are the result of her ignorance and romanticism; the idea that she is attracted by his difference and her romantic fantasies about the African Prince.

Pages 26–27
Quick Test
1. Helen
2. Through her drawings
3. The Boy (Jimmie)

Exam Practice

Answers might refer to her mixture of youthful innocence and maturity; her neglect by Helen; her attitude to Helen; her use of ironic humour; her determination to leave school; her sense of independence; her curiosity about the world; her fear of the dark; her need to be loved; her jealousy; her aggression; her changeability.

Analysis might include the way in which discussion of Jo's drawings turns into an argument when she answers Helen's question with 'I'm never at one school long enough', which Helen takes as an accusation; Jo's use of the formal 'Mister Smith' to provoke Peter and the sexual implication of her questions, 'do I bother you?' and 'must I wait until we're alone?'; the way he responds by asking Helen to control her; the implication that she knows the Boy is unreliable but is more interested in the present and her moment of happiness than in the future.

Pages 28–29
Quick Test
1. Geof
2. A baby doll
3. She now says she does not want to marry.
4. She accepts her help.

Exam Practice

Answers might refer to changes since Act 1; her feelings about pregnancy; her neglect of herself and her flat; her jobs and attitude to money; her changeability and depression; her assertion of her independence and strength; her light moments with Geof; her stubbornness; her humour; her resilience.

Analysis might include Jo's response of 'I'm feeling nothing' suggesting that Geof is right to think she is depressed; her use of the more formal 'Geoffrey' to admonish Geof; her assertion of independence in 'I'm not having anybody running my life for me' contradicted by her increasing reliance on Geof; her later assertion of her own independence and ability and the implication that the prospect of having a baby is giving her a purpose in life; the possibility that – given what we know of her so far – the audience might doubt her ability to take care of anyone, including herself.

Pages 30–31

Quick Test

1. In pubs
2. She says she is 'careful'.
3. To go away with Peter.
4. She wants to help her and she has nowhere else to live.

Exam Practice

Answers might refer to her selfishness; her enjoyment of life, including drink and sex; her lack of a sense of responsibility; her materialism; her fatalism; her ironic humour; her optimism; her resilience.

Analysis might include Jo's accusations of selfishness, which repeat the **second person** and use the **antonyms** 'always' and 'never' to stress that Helen has not changed and her behaviour does not change; Helen's reference to her 'suffering' being notable because she does not usually complain about things; her use of a humorous insult to downplay Peter's unfaithfulness; her use of the common phrase 'it was good while it lasted' to suggest that she does not dwell on bad experiences.

Pages 32–33

Quick Test

1. He lost his eye during the war.
2. That he has had a lot of girlfriends.
3. Aggressively/offensively

Exam Practice

Answers might refer to the way he pursues and courts her; the age difference; the way he buys her presents; their crude jokes and innuendoes; their drinking; Jo's feelings about the relationship; his unfaithfulness.

Analysis might include his vanity in talking about his marriage proposal as an 'opportunity' for Helen, though this may be ironic; his boastful use of the image of the world being 'littered with women' he has rejected and the idea that Helen might find this flattering; Jo's direct question to Helen showing her suspicion of the relationship; Helen's use of the **metaphor** of a wallet being a joke but at the same time showing her materialism and suggesting she might be motivated by money rather than love; Peter's use of the metaphor of the gutter implying that he looks down on Helen and that he feels he has done her a favour.

Pages 34–35

Quick Test

1. He is doing National Service.
2. A ring
3. He will return and he will marry her.
4. That he is an African prince.

Exam Practice

Answers might refer to his race; his awareness of racism; his feelings for Jo; his light-hearted flirting; his proposal of marriage; his care for Jo when she is left alone; his references to *Othello*; his sexual drive; his promise to return; his failure to return; Jo's fantasy of him as an African prince; her reaction to his abandonment.

Analysis might include his use of the adjective 'afraid' in his question to Jo, suggesting he thinks she might be concerned about his race; her reply showing her attitude; his use of 'taking advantage' (a euphemism for having sex) and 'scruples' to suggest he respects Jo; the flirtatious and perhaps

ironic tone of those statements; his jokey and flirtatious use of the formal 'dishonourable intentions' and her immediate positive response showing her desire to have sex with him.

Pages 36–37

Quick Test

1. He thinks they are sentimental.
2. Three from: buys a book about babies, gets her a doll, buys a cot, does the housework, makes clothes.
3. Helen

Exam Practice

Answers might refer to the platonic nature of the relationship; his sexuality; her calling him a 'big sister'; his criticism of her art; his desire to help her; the practical ways in which he helps; his kiss and Jo's rejection; his assertion that he could not live without her; his fetching of Helen; his selfless act in leaving the flat.

Analysis might include his sensitivity when he thinks he is being laughed at; his concern shown in his question to Jo; the verb 'manage' meaning both manage financially and cope emotionally; his persistence when she brushes off his question; the reason given for his desire to help; Jo's use of the word 'always' to show the strength of her feelings; the sense that her feelings towards him have deepened; the superficial meaning of him not wanting anything from her being that he does not want a sexual relationship; the phrase also meaning that he is undemanding; a sense that this statement is about her needs and not his; the irony in the fact that he leaves soon afterwards.

Pages 38–39

Quick Test

1. She is angry.
2. She thinks it will be born 'dead or daft' if she does.
3. Geof

Exam Practice

Answers might explore Jo's ambivalence; her refusal to consider abortion; her refusal to plan for the birth; Geof's idea that she is depressed; her reaction to the baby doll and the book about babies; her talk of the baby being dead and her killing it; talk of leaving the baby on a doorstep; her acceptance of Geof's help; her fear of the birth; her claim that she feels powerful and can take care of everyone.

Analysis might include the casualness of Geof's suggestion about abortion; Jo's instant rejection of the idea; her use of the word 'terrible' without further explanation or discussion; the contrast between this and her later feelings of violence towards the baby; her use of the imperative 'shut up' to avoid discussion of the future; the **parallel phrasing** ('planning big plans ... dreaming big dreams') and repetition of 'big' as she explains why she will not discuss it and what her reason for this tells us about her fear and her pessimistic attitude; how Helen's exclamation comically reflects traditional ideas about who should be at a birth.

Pages 40–41

Quick Test

1. She praises her drawings; she asks about her boyfriend.
2. No
3. She thinks Jo will need her when she has the baby.

Exam Practice

Answers might refer to their constant arguing and whether they enjoy it; Helen's lack of responsibility; Jo blaming Helen for neglecting her; their similarities and differences; the centrality of their relationship to the play.

Analysis might include Jo's anger and resentment in her summary of Helen's attitude to her; Helen's use of irony in her response; Helen's failure to deny the accusation; the fact that they shout at each other, as reinforced by Geof's question; Helen's claim that they enjoy it being comic but possibly true; Jo finishing Helen's sentence and following it with an accusation of neglect in the form of a rhetorical question.

Pages 42–43

Quick Test

1. A ring
2. By giving her presents and taking her out.
3. Geof and Jo's

Exam Practice

Answers might refer to Jo's desire to be loved; the love between Jo and the Boy; her doubts about whether it was love; Helen's cynicism about love; Helen and Peter's relationship and whether they love each other; Geof's love for Jo.

Analysis might include Helen's reference to a diamond ring as a symbol of marriage with the implication that she is more interested in its monetary value; Peter's half-joking half-serious response showing that he too is cynical about love; Jo's unemotional summary of how her background was loveless and therefore she is not sure if she was in love; Helen's view of Jo's love affair and Jo's response; how the insulting language used to describe Jo suggests it was all about sex and not love.

Pages 44–45

Quick Test

1. He is in the Royal Navy and he has friends in the Navy.
2. She is not prejudiced/she is attracted to them.
3. His eye patch

Exam Practice

Answers might explore the way Helen and Jo move frequently; how they do not settle anywhere and so do not 'belong'; the Boy's race and origins; Jo's interest in him as an outsider and her romantic ideas about his origins; Geof's sexuality making him an outsider; Geof and Jo enjoying the idea of being misfits and outside normal society.

Analysis might include Jo's repetition of 'too many' suggesting she is tired of not belonging; her rejection of the Boy's 'ordinary' background as she prefers the more exotic idea of the 'jungle'; how her remarks show she is drawn to him partly because he is different; the nouns 'beggars' and 'degenerates' used by Jo to describe her and Geof as misfits; the use of 'we' and 'a couple' to link them; Geof's exclamation embracing their status as misfits.

Pages 46–47

Quick Test

1. Helen
2. By marrying Peter.
3. Clothes and make-up
4. Geof

Exam Practice

Answers might refer to the way Jo and Helen's poverty is established in the exposition; Jo blaming Helen for their situation; Helen's route out of poverty via Peter; Jo's jobs; her situation at the beginning of Act 2; her inability to manage money; Geof's support.

Analysis might include Jo's immediate negative reaction to the flat; the parallel phrasing of Helen's reply; Jo's answer to Geof implying that 'all I need' does not include real necessities such as food and rent; Helen's lack of sympathy when talking to Geof about Jo and her use of a **simile** ('like a little bloodsucker') that shows she does not approve of Geof supporting Jo and thinks Jo should take responsibility.

Pages 48–49

Quick Test

1. Bulbs
2. Through drawing/art
3. Touching up photographs.
4. By making wicker baskets.

Exam Practice

Answers might include references to Jo's drawings and Helen's and Geof's differing reactions to them; the idea that creativity needs to be trained; Geof's use of his talents to help Jo; the woman downstairs making baskets; Jo's identification of birth with creativity.

Analysis might include Helen's inability to praise Jo without insulting her as well; Helen's characteristic use of humour; Geof turning the drawings into a symbol of Jo's character and his use of the terminology of the art class; Jo's use of a generalised saying to tell Geof about her pregnancy; her self-deprecating humour.

Pages 50–51

Quick Test

1. The slaughterhouse
2. A coffin
3. By bashing its brains out.

Exam Practice

Answers might refer to Jo being afraid of the dark; the darkness in the flat; the distinction Jo makes between darkness inside and outside; Helen's contrasting attitude; the darkness of winter; the dark as somewhere to hide; keeping the flat dark in Act 2; growing the bulbs in the dark; darkness associated with the Boy.

Analysis might include the association of darkness and fear; Helen's implication that Jo can overcome her fear herself; Jo's use of the simile 'black as coal' associating the Boy with darkness through his skin colour; the contrast between the prosaic 'coal' and the exotic 'darkest Africa', both expressions being stereotypical; the association of darkness with mystery in 'darkest Africa'.

Pages 52–53

Quick Test

1. Her relationship with the Boy
2. No
3. Her relationship with Peter
4. Her relationship with Jo's father

Exam Practice

Answers might refer to the contrast between Jo's scenes with the Boy and her relationship with Helen; Helen's attitude to pleasure and her own actions; Jo and the Boy's declarations of love; her invitation to him to stay; her desire to sleep with him; her awareness that he might not come back; Helen's anger at Jo's 'waste' of her life; the consequence of the 'taste of honey' in her pregnancy and her lack of regret.

Analysis might include Jo's use of the childish adjective 'naughty', reflecting a sense that she is doing something wrong but not serious; her sudden change of mood; the implied fatalism of saying she will not see him again; the way in which this knowledge does not change her actions; Helen's sudden anger with Jo and the awareness that her own 'taste of honey' with Jo's father was similar to Jo's affair with the Boy.

Pages 54–55

Quick Test

1. Irony
2. The prospect of the birth of her baby.
3. She thinks she exaggerates and feels sorry for herself.
4. Helen

Exam Practice

Answers might refer to her lack of concern about the state of the flat and neighbourhood; her use of ironic humour; her attitude to her past problems; her enjoyment of life; her optimism; her return after Peter's unfaithfulness; her lack of bitterness about the relationship.

Analysis might include her dismissal of Jo's ideas with the phrase 'funny ideas'; her direct address to the audience in 'Listen to it!' as if sharing a joke with them; the light humorous tone of her remarks; her generalisation of 'we all'; the fatalism implied in 'end up the same way'; her downplaying of Jo's situation with her ironic hyperbolic use of 'tragedy queen'; her refusal to feel sorry for Jo; her direct no-nonsense command.

Pages 56–57

Quick Test

1. Female
2. They are low paid and without prospects.
3. Peter and the Boy
4. Shopping, housework, sewing

Exam Practice

Answers might refer to the secondary nature of the male characters; their unreliability; the idea that they are less mature than women; the sense that they have more money and opportunities than women; the way both Helen and Jo accept support from men; Geof taking on a mixture of traditionally male and traditionally female roles.

Analysis might include Jo's association of the Boy with 'little boys', suggesting she feels he and other men are immature; the phrase's patronising tone; the **pejorative** noun 'trash' used of his possessions; Geof's feeling that women and men are very different; the implication that men cannot understand women.

Pages 60–61

Use the mark scheme below to self-assess your strengths and weaknesses. The estimated grade boundaries are included so you can assess your progress towards your target grades.

Pages 62–63

Quick Test

1. Understanding of the whole text; specific analysis and terminology; awareness of the relevance of context; a well-structured essay and accurate writing.

2. Planning focuses your thoughts and helps you to produce a well-structured essay.
3. Quotations give you opportunities to do specific AO2 analysis.

Exam Practice

Answers might include: Helen's independence; her resilience; the ways in which she copes with financial and emotional difficulties; her reaction to Jo's pregnancy; her reaction to Peter's affair; her ironic sense of humour; her acceptance of adversity; her ability to 'bounce back'; her fatalistic approach to life; her enjoyment of life; her lack of bitterness; and what the future might hold for her.

Pages 66–67 and 72–73

Use the mark scheme below to self-assess your strengths and weaknesses. Work up from the bottom, putting a tick by things you have fully accomplished, a ½ by skills that are in place but need developing, and underlining areas that have not been covered or need particular development. The estimated grade boundaries are included so you can assess your progress towards your target grades.

Pages 68–69

Quick Test

1. Understanding of the whole text; specific analysis and terminology; awareness of the relevance of context; a well-structured essay and accurate writing.

2. Planning focuses your thoughts and helps you to produce a well-structured essay.
3. Quotations give you opportunities to do specific AO2 analysis.

Exam Practice

Answers might include: the way in which Jo is let down by Helen and the Boy; Helen is let down by Peter and her marriage ends badly; the circular structure; the lack of ambition in Jo; lack of opportunity; the depressing setting; Jo's confidence that she can cope at the end; the hope of a new birth; Jo and Helen's resilience; Jo's rejection of prejudice; the way in which the characters 'get on with life'.

Grade	AO1	AO2	AO3	AO4
6–7+	A convincing and well-structured essay that answers the question fully. Quotations and references are well-chosen and integrated into sentences. The response covers the whole play.	Analysis of the full range of Delaney's methods. Thorough exploration of the effects of these methods. Range of accurate subject terminology.	Exploration is linked to specific aspects of the play's contexts to show detailed understanding.	Consistently high level of accuracy. Vocabulary and sentences are used to make ideas clear and precise.
4–5	A clear essay that always focuses on the question. Quotations and references support ideas effectively. The response refers to different points in the play.	Explanation of Delaney's different methods. Clear understanding of the effects of these methods. Accurate use of subject terminology.	References to relevant aspects of context show clear understanding.	Good level of accuracy. Vocabulary and sentences help to keep ideas clear.
2–3	The essay has some good ideas that are mostly relevant. Some quotations and references are used to support ideas.	Identification of some different methods used by Delaney to convey meaning. Some subject terminology.	Some awareness of how ideas in the play link to its context.	Reasonable level of accuracy. Errors do not get in the way of the essay making sense.